No Greater Loss

The Handbook to Today's Grandparents' Rights

Neil Taft

No Greater Loss

Copyright © 2010 by Neil Taft

"Neil Taft, in his usual enthusiastic manner, has written a book that can effectively guide grandparents in the many decisions they must make so that their rights are maintained while still ensuring benefits that are in the best interest of their grandchildren."

Laurie Renz Ph.D.

Professor Emeritus, University of Cincinnati

"Remember, if death takes a grandparent from a grandchild, that is a tragedy, but if petty vindictiveness and hostilities within a family amputate a grandchild from their grandparents, then that is a shame."

Richard S. Victor

founder and executive director national nonprofit Grandparents' rights Organization

Preface

Congratulations. You have arrived at this page because you are a **Caring Grandparent**. You will find that I have written this book to help bridge the gap between Logic and Law. Grandparents have provided and still provide so much caring continuity in our extended families…and yet there is a danger that these relationships are being lost to misdirected anger and vindictiveness by irrational people in the process of fracturing the family unit. This upheaval is happening at precisely the time when our grandchildren need a steady, caring hand to reassure them. Like you, I feel very strongly about the best interest of our grandchildren.

To be clear, nothing about grandparents' rights as presented here is intended in any way to dilute or challenge any rights of a FIT parent. I believe that a grandparent's primary role in the extended functioning family is to support and enhance the role of the parent(s).

Two major factors have prompted this work.

1. Our divorce rate is near 50 percent.

2. The United States Constitution addresses parental rights in three different sections (as it surely should) but there is no mention of grandparents' rights.

Divorce is about so many things, most of which are highly emotional, and it leaves wounded soldiers in its path. Most times the children experience some, if not many, negative consequences in the process. Unfortunately, grandparents who can contribute to healing these hurting grandchildren are often thrown under the bus for reasons that defy logic.

There are many theories and reasons given as to why grandparents' rights were not in the Constitution, but we will never know the answers. This powerful force for good (grandparents make up one-third of the adult population of this country) is made to turn to the state legislatures for legal protection of their long-standing and morally appropriate rights. All 50 states have grandparents' rights legislation in some form, but as you can imagine there is a great variety of language and interpretation of these many laws.

As if these are not enough reasons there remains one reason to embrace grandparents' rights that shines above all: **the children**. This entire volume is credited to and dedicated to my six wonderful Grand Angels, who are so much a part of who I am that they define me in many ways. Children deserve all of our energy and caring to help them grow up to be loving and lovable members of this great society.

Thanks for Caring,
GRANDPA NEIL
www.caringgrandparents.com

Foreword

Children are our legacy and the future. They need all of the resources, encouragement, and belief in their abilities that can be provided to them. Grandparents are a good source for this encouragement and can contribute greatly to their growth and development. In fact, grandparents have experience and knowledge to share that they learned in life and from decisions they made, good and bad, which brought them to their present state.

Learning what rights and privileges grandparents have adds to the understanding of all family members and strengthens the family unit. It informs and helps in dealing with simple and complex issues that arise in the lives of all children. Navigating through difficulties is easier with some help from the more experienced. Learning methods of coping is a valuable skill. To witness mastery of new learning is a joy anyone can appreciate.

Reading this book will add dimensions to your knowledge base and will help you to help a child. No other job is as rewarding and as vitally important as our investment in tomorrow. Assisting a child to grow in competence in small things leads to increased abilities in decision making on a larger scale. As you grow in understanding your rights with your grandchildren you will become a better grandparent. Once on this path you will find yourself anxious to stay a part of the process of unlimited human potential.

Neil is the product of great love and great sorrow, having been adored by his mother and abandoned through death by his father at age eleven. It is this combination that has made him extremely sensitive to the issues in this book. He has mentored more young people than can be counted and as a grandparent to six he thrives on instilling positive attitudes and creativity to all children. His passion for grandparents' rights cannot be doubted.

There are many different directions available for families to go, but to see grandparents cut off from their grandchildren is a terrible path to witness. Instead, children need the warmth, acceptance, and love that grandparents offer. You can be a catalyst for those gifts and help guide the course of these little people making this a better life in a better world. Neil is a great guide to help get you there.

Dr. Susanne Taft, Psychologist

Table of Contents

1

www.caringgrandparents.com

An Overview of Grandparents' Rights

"Perfect love sometimes does not come until that first grandchild."

Welsh Proverb

Many people unfamiliar with the issues surrounding grandparents' rights may assume that grandparents automatically have the rights and access to their grandchildren that they should. In truth, grandparents do not have these rights unless they are permitted by the parents or unless grandparents win them through the legal system.

In most cases, if parents recognize that grandparents should morally have the right to see their grandchildren and be an integral part of their lives, it is the best of all outcomes for the family and especially for the children. In such cases, the children enormously benefit from what the grandparents bring to their lives, and the grandparents also benefit from having a close relationship with their grandchildren.

The reality of life is that it is complicated. The reality of family is that it is a multiple of complicated and the reality of extended family is that it is exponentially complicated. And if those aren't enough factors we need to recognize that over 50 percent of all marriages today end in divorce. Given these layers of complexity there needs to be a way for each family member to contribute to the best interest of the children without taking away from others in the family, especially fit parents.

I don't want to lose sight of the fact that most grandparent/grandchildren relationships are healthy and productive and do much to add value to the family unit. We find that most times the grandparents will enjoy wonderful and mutually fruitful relationships with several of their grandkids, but that one arm of the extended family is in crisis and that is when trouble surfaces. The sad part is that it is the loss that weighs most heavily on the grandparents' minds. They instinctively know this is precisely the time that their grandchildren need them the most.

As I have written many times, parents' rights are protected (and rightfully so) in three separate places in the Constitution of these United States. I am not sure if it was for reasons of short life expectancy at the time of the writing of the Constitution or the time constraints on getting it done or the climate of parent/grandparent cooperation that existed. For whatever reasons the founding fathers didn't anticipate the complications of our modern-day society. If they had I am sure they would have expounded on the rights of grandparents for all the same reasons they assured the rights of the parents. Well, we "couldna-shoulda-been there" so we will never know.

If the grandparents find they are shut out of their grandchildren's lives today then they may have to go to court to have their grandparents' rights upheld, and that is a very difficult and demanding process.

In the United States every single state has separate statutes that give permission to the grandparents to maintain contact with their grandchildren. But though all fifty states have regulations on grandparents' legal rights, they vary considerably on procedures and practices. This handbook will help you with that journey.

Grandparents' Rights Today

Grandparents have always had limited rights to visitation and custody of their grandchildren, and in 2000 the U.S. Supreme Court limited these rights even further through its decision in the case of Troxell v. Granville (you will read much more on this important decision later). Currently the laws vary in each state. It is important to understand, however, that there are still some situations where a grandparent may have legal rights regarding a grandchild.

Although a grandparent in many states lacks the ability to petition the court for custody of a grandchild, it may be possible to do so on a temporary basis in an emergency situation. This situation most commonly occurs when a parent passes away but may also take place in other situations such as when the legal parents are unable to adequately care for their children due to incarceration, drug use, or military deployment.

A grandparent can petition the courts for guardianship of a grandchild if there is an emergency to justify it, the parental rights of the parents have been terminated, or if the child has been living with the grandparents for an extended period of time due to the lack of care by the child's parents. Although being appointed as a guardian does not automatically include legal custody, guardians are eligible to petition the court for full custody of a child.

Grandparents' visitation rights is one area where grandparents can petition the court to give them access to the child in most any state. Typically, in order for the court to grant visitation to the grandparents, they must establish that the parents of the child are either divorced, separated or are planning to divorce, or that the child's parent has passed away.

The Troxel Case and Grandparents' Rights

Anyone interested and involved with grandparents' rights needs to be aware of the Troxel case and its subsequent implications on grandparents' rights. The Supreme Court issued this ruling with a 6-3 decision in June of 2000. It cancelled out a state law in Washington which permitted courts to grant visitation rights to any interested party as long as it was in the best interest of the child.

Troxel v. Granville came about in 1993 when two grandparents asked for visitation with two grandchildren, who were in the custody of their son's estranged girlfriend after his suicide. The grandparents, Gary and Jennifer Troxel, sued for visitation rights based on the Washington state law, claiming that they had the right to visitation as long as it was in the best interests of their grandchildren.

The Troxels won additional visitation rights in court but the Supreme Court eventually invalidated the trial court's decision and declared the Washington state law was unconstitutional, as it was too broad and it infringed upon parents' rights.

The Supreme Court decision in Troxel, however, was ambiguous and difficult to interpret because the six justices who sided against grandparents' rights had six different reasons for doing so, resulting in six different opinions.

Grandparents' Rights After Troxel

Although the Troxel case only cancelled out the Washington state law, other states have tried to refer to it in figuring out if their own state laws regarding grandparents' rights are constitutional. Many states have amended or rewritten their statutes in the wake of Troxel.

This has led to a hodgepodge of state laws without uniform guidance on a national level. Grandparents are allowed to file for both visitation and custody post-Troxel, but whether they are successful or not depends upon the specific laws of the state they file in (all court cases must be heard in the state where the child resides).

Generally after Troxel, all states require that grandparents be able to prove that the visitation they seek is in the best interest of the child. Some states are even more restrictive, allowing grandparents to file for visitation only after they have been totally shut out of the grandchildren's lives. In a few of the most restrictive states, grandparents must prove that they have previously acted as a parent to the child.

The Problem with Restricting Grandparents' Rights Since Troxel

Paradoxically, in the time since the Troxel case was decided grandparents have become even more important in our society. Times of recession, skyrocketing divorce rates, and war have fostered the need for grandparents to often take an even more active role in their grandchildren's lives, as family needs and dynamics have shifted.

Societal problems such as drug and alcohol abuse, child abuse, absent parents, and poverty have seen grandparents step up the already powerful commitment they make to their grandchildren. Current estimates are that over six million children in the USA live in a grandparent's household away from their parents, and in one-half of these households have no parent present.

Yet our laws have not kept up with these changes, and while grandparents have even that much more importance in our society they have been denied the common-sense rights that should go along with this importance.

Grandparents Still Do Have Rights!

Despite questionable court decisions and laws every state still has some form of grandparents' visitation statute, and in many cases you as a grandparent may have the right to file for visitation or even custody. The next two chapters deal with the specifics of grandparents' visitation and grandparents' custody, so read on to find out how to enforce the rights that grandparents are still allowed in our society.

2

Grandparents' Visitation: Answers You Need

"Grandparents make the world…a little softer, a little kinder, a little warmer."

Author Unknown

In this chapter you'll find important answers to some of the urgent questions most often asked by grandparents seeking visitation rights with their grandchildren.

There are as many questions as there are circumstances but this gives you a good cross section of subjects that attract the most questions. You will find additional resources in our later section by that name, as well as some direction to getting specific answers to your specific questions through our website www.caringgrandparents.com. The purpose of this section is to offer food for thought and give you a sense that you are not plowing new ground. There are pioneers in this field of law that can and will help you through this difficult time.

It is important to understand that differing states have different grandparents' visitation laws on the books. The last national ruling on grandparents' visitation rights was in the 2000 Supreme Court case of Troxel v. Granville.

The Troxel case reaffirmed the rights of parents under the 14th Amendment and set the standard that in grandparents' rights cases, fit parents are presumed to be acting in the best interest of the child. This has made filing and winning visitation for grandparents more difficult, but not impossible. Now is the time for some true soul-searching. Please don't shoot the messenger, but it is paramount that you really, really consider two questions here:

Why am I really doing this?

And…

What is at stake if I go to this next step?

There are no answers from me, only guidelines. On this first point I am reminded of what a very good friend once asked: "How much do you want to pay to be right?" While the amount of money you will spend is significant it pales in comparison to the cost to the extended family members and family unity as a whole. This is the perfect time for me to remind you, "It is all about the children."

I definitely don't ask these questions to discourage you from going forward. I truly believe that if after honestly considering your motivations you find it in the best interest of your grandchildren, then I encourage action and I would encourage you if the kids are old enough to understand that you be honest and share with them that you are doing this with them in mind.

The second question is related to motives but it goes a step further; it goes to the most effective way to accomplish what we think is the right thing to do. In the section on best practices I encourage negotiation and if that doesn't work I encourage negotiation, etc. You get the picture. After all that I would encourage mediation if it is appropriate. Only then should you avail yourself of your legal grandparents' rights.

The questions this chapter answers are:

1. Should I consider filing for visitation with my grandchildren?

2. What are some valid reasons to file for visitation with my grandchildren?

3. What circumstances may prevent me from filing for visitation with my grandchildren?

4. Should I hire an attorney?

5. Are grandparents ever awarded visitation with their grandchildren? (Yes, lots.)

....

1. Should I consider filing for visitation with my grandchildren?

Some amount of conflict between parents and grandparents over the raising of children is common. If you are having difficulty seeing your grandchildren, the first (and second) option should be to attempt to negotiate and mediate a compromise with the parents.

If you can avoid going to court you should do so. There is much more information on reasons not to go to court and how to handle disputes in the chapter on best practices (problem prevention) and avoiding the courtroom.

There you find that I first advocate using any and all problem-solving best practices in order to avoid coming to the point you need to involve the courts. If, however, you have deemed compromise truly impossible in the situation, you can seek court-ordered visitation in many cases.

2. What are some valid reasons to file for visitation?

You will need a valid and compelling reason to file for visitation rights with your grandchildren. Simply having disagreements with the way your grandchildren are being raised does not qualify as a valid reason. You must have been seriously cut-off from your grandchildren and have attempted all informal means of remedying the situation within the family.

Valid reasons for a grandparent to be granted visitation that have the potential to be upheld in court include:

You are not allowed visitation with your grandchildren after a divorce.

This unfortunate circumstance occurs when the parent gaining custody of your grandchild after a divorce is not your own child, and does not wish to maintain contact between you and your grandchild. In this case, you may have no choice but to file for court-ordered visitation. Although there is no guarantee, courts have been sensitive to grandparents in this position in many states.

Death of one or more of the child's parents.

In the case of the death of one parent of the child, you may run into a situation like the one above regarding divorce. If the surviving parent is not your child and does not wish to allow you to see your grandchild (or see them with any regularity at all) you may have to file for court-ordered visitation if you hope to be in their lives. Here again, some state courts have been sympathetic to grandparents in this position.

It may be even more important to go to the courts in the unfortunate case of the death of both your grandchild's parents. If a child is adopted by someone else you generally lose all of your grandparents' rights regarding visitation (the child is no longer considered your grandchild legally).

Here you might consider filing for custody, as grandparents' visitation is no longer a possibility after an adoption. See the chapter on grandparent custody for more information if you fall into this category.

Also remember that you can still informally work out visitation with a child's adopted family and that is a far better option than going to court if it is available to you. You should also know that a positive side to adoption is that if your child adopts, you have all of the normal grandparents' rights with that child, including seeking court-ordered visitation if the circumstances apply.

Your grandchild's non-custodial parent (your child) does not exercise his/her visitation rights.

If your child has visitation with his/her children but for some reason is unable to or refuses to exercise these visitation rights, you may petition the court for grandparents' visitation on the basis that the child is being denied a sense of family. Again, while there are no guarantees, courts in many states have been sympathetic to grandparents making the argument that some visitation from their side of the family is in a child's best interest.

Parental instability.

If there are severe problems regarding parental stability, such as emotional problems, drug or alcohol use, neglect, or severe financial issues, you may be able to obtain grandparents' visitation from the court if the parent is not allowing you visitation. Grandparents may ask the courts to order visitation as a way of "checking up" on your grandchildren and judging whether more extreme measures need to be taken.

Unfortunately, in most states even in these circumstances grandparents may not have the right to visitation if the grandchild's parents are still married and living together (see below).

Keep in mind that whether or not court-ordered visitation is available to you, if you become aware of serious threats to your grandchild such as abuse or severe neglect you should immediately go to authorities so that the matter can be investigated and you can ensure the safety of your grandchild.

You have been acting as a parent to the child.

There have been cases where a grandparent was, for some reason, acting as a parent to a grandchild due to the parent's inability or unwillingness to do so. After a parent resumed their normal custody with the child the grandparents had to petition the courts to allow them visitation, and the courts did so based of the extraordinary nature of the grandparent's previous contact with the child.

This is a narrow category but if you fall into it (and are unable to negotiate visitation with the parent after trying) you may meet the court's standard for visitation rights based on what your relationship with your grandchild has been.

3. What circumstances may prevent me from filing for visitation with my grandchildren?

There are both informal and legal reasons that you may decide not to file for visitation even if you are unhappy with the situation as it stands now.

Informal reasons not to file for visitation.

These are common sense reasons that you may decide filing for visitation is a bad idea. Generally, taking your grandchild's parent to court will cause conflict and animosity between you and the parent that you may wish to avoid, and that should be factored into your decision.

You must also decide if a court case regarding visitation, with the potential for conflict and emotion that it brings, is in the best interest of your grandchild. Finally, visitation court cases involve substantial commitments of time, money, and emotion you may not be willing to make.

All of these informal reasons not to file for court-ordered visitation must be weighed against the possible gain. There is much more information on reasons not to go to court and how to handle disputes in the chapters on problem prevention and avoiding the courtroom.

Your grandchild's parents are presently married and living together.

In most states you are not eligible to file for grandparents visitation if your grandchild's parents are presently married and still living together. In the states that do allow you to file there is usually a tougher standard to meet in these cases, such as proving you had previous "extraordinary contact" with your grandchildren.

In most cases, grandparents wishing visitation (or more frequent visitation) in situations where the grandchildren's parents are married and living together are usually better off seeking it outside of the courtroom.

There is evidence you have been abusive to a child.

If there is any substantial evidence that you have been physically, emotionally, or sexually abusive to any child the court is unlikely to grant you visitation even if you qualify. In some states a conviction for child abuse automatically prevents you from filing for visitation, but in any case courts are not likely to rule visitation with you is in the best interest of the child.

If these legal standards do not apply to you and you have carefully weighed the informal reasons not to proceed with a court case, you will most likely be eligible to file for grandparents' visitation.

4. Should I hire an attorney?

In general, in most cases where you as the grandparent are seeking visitation with your grandchildren you will want to hire an attorney to represent you in court. This is due to an attorney's familiarity with the laws in the state where your grandchild resides, and with the court system and judges.

What is at stake?

You must also consider what is at stake if you are able to bring a visitation suit but lose the case. In this circumstance not only will you be denied court-ordered visitation but you will still have to deal with all of the informal problems with going to court, such as the animosity of your grandchild's parents.

Bringing a grandparents visitation suit but losing it makes it unlikely the parent will voluntarily give you visitation in the future. Therefore, if you bring a grandparents visitation suit you need to have a reasonable expectation of winning, and consulting and/or hiring an attorney can prove invaluable in measuring the risks and rewards of your particular case.

In most cases hiring an attorney to represent you in court gives you the best chance of winning your court-ordered grandparents' visitation rights.

5. Are grandparents ever awarded visitation with their grandchildren? (Good news, the answer is yes in many cases)

You must remember that, fairly or unfairly, the burden of proof is on you as the grandparent in all cases of visitation regardless of the circumstances. You must overcome the presumption of the courts that fit parents are acting in the best interests of the child.

While that may seem daunting, the fact is that grandparents bring visitation cases to the courts and are awarded visitation rights all the time. If you are being kept from seeing your grandchild and have done everything reasonably possible outside of court to remedy the situation, then seeking court-ordered grandparents' visitation is your right.

3

Grandparents' Custody: Questions You Need to Ask, and Answers

"Grandparents are the footsteps to the future generations."

Author Unknown

The Constitution of the United States rightfully protects, in three separate sections, the right of **"fit"** parents to raise their children as they judge to be best for the children. Thankfully, in the greatest majority of cases this is hugely successful and results in neat and wonderful young minds developing and contributing to society. However, that word **"fit"** is paramount in these constitutional premises. Unfortunately, some parents get caught up in their own stuff and can't or won't protect and nurture their children. The Caring Grandparent is usually the first to notice and best equipped to intervene.

This is the chapter where "the rubber hits the road." Only committed, responsible, Caring Grandparents would consider reentering the ranks of parenting again to rescue their grandchildren. While there is some crossover to the previous chapter's questions and answers this is a situation where the courts will definitely be involved. This is not a do-it-yourself project. I encourage you to find a good attorney early on in this process.

In an attempt to decrease some of your apprehension I will let you know there are, sadly, over 6 million grandchildren being raised in their grandparents' homes, and in half those homes neither parent is residing in the home with the kids. As noble and heroic as these grandparents are, there is NOTHING easy about these situations. Please take a moment and celebrate the fact that you are loving and brave enough to even consider this path. Now let us get about providing you the information and resources to help you decide the best course for your grandchild as well as you.

There is no group of people more qualified and positioned to guard and protect the best interests of grandchildren than their extended family. As tragic as the disintegration of the family unit is the damage would be multiplied if not for a Caring Grandparent willing to step forward to rescue a grandchild.

As you consider your rights as a grandparent under the law I would ask that you be honest with yourself about how profoundly this decision will change your life. I also encourage you to avail yourself of ALL of the support and help available to guide you through this maze. As an aside I have found a book that is listed in the resource section on the website www.caringgrandparents.com called *A KINSHIP Guide to Rescuing Children* by Helene LaBrecque Ellis. Helene will give you a quick and concise look at what help is available to you and more important how to get at that help. There are many other sources of information and support and as more current information becomes available we will share that with everyone on our website.

In this chapter you'll find important answers to some of the urgent questions most often asked by grandparents seeking custody of their grandchild.

Keep in mind this information assumes that you are seeking permanent custody and not temporary custody (which occurs under different circumstances and in which the courts use different standards). Also, remember that the laws and procedures vary from state to state and any custody cases will take place in the state where the child resides.

The questions this chapter answers are:

1. Do I qualify for filing for custody of my grandchildren?

2. What criteria are used to determine custody for my grandchildren?

3. What circumstances can be used to my advantage in filing for custody?

4. What factors can be used against me in filing for custody?

5. Should I hire an attorney?

6. Are grandparents ever awarded custody of their grandchildren? (Yes, lots.)

. . . .

1. Do I qualify for filing for custody of my grandchild?

All states have conditions that grandparents must fall under in order to petition for legal custody of their grandchildren. Many states set these as a list of requirements, but they are fairly uniform no matter which state you live in.

The most obvious and number one requirement that you must fulfill when seeking custody is that you be able to establish in court that you have had enough substantial past contact to constitute a significant pre-existing relationship with your grandchildren.

Although the exact definition of "significant pre-existing relationship" may vary from state to state, case to case, or even judge to judge, courts usually use common sense to determine whether or not your past relationship with your grandchildren is substantial.

If you have seen your grandchild regularly and have been a part of their lives, you probably fulfill this and other basic requirements for filing for custody of your grandchild. Only if there are large gaps in your participation in their lives, or a judge believes you have intentionally avoided being part of their lives, is there a likelihood you will not meet the qualifications for filing for custody.

If, however, you have been willing to see your grandchild but not allowed, that can be considered by the court to be a circumstance in your favor.

2. What criteria are used to determine custody for my grandchildren?

Parental preference.

States generally use one of two standards for determining custody. The courts in many states currently begin any proceedings by looking for the parental preference, meaning that the wishes of the child's parents will be followed unless there is strongly significant evidence to the court that they should not be respected.

The reason for this is that the Constitution gives a fit parent the right to determine what is best for the well-being of their child. Generally a grandparent then has the responsibility in overcoming parental preference by proving the parents are (to a great degree) unfit to have custody of their own children before the court will consider the grandparents for custody.

Best interest of the child.

States without a disposition toward parental preference generally try to follow the best interest of the child as the decisive factor in granting custody. Although this is not as difficult a standard for grandparents to overcome as parental preference it still means that you may have to prove why a parent is largely unfit to have custody while supporting your own claim.

In the Troxel v. Granville case, however, the Supreme Court made it clear that the best interest of the child should not be the sole reason (or only factor) for granting custody.

3. What circumstances can be used to my advantage in filing for custody?

Overcoming the courts' natural predisposition to granting or maintaining parental custody means that you will have to show some factors or conditions that prove that your grandchild's parent is unfit. It is not enough to simply suspect (or even know these things) but you also must be able to present evidence that proves them to a judge in court.

Parental abuse or neglect.

The most serious allegation that you can attempt to prove in court is that of abuse or neglect of the child. Therefore, if you make this allegation you can expect a spirited denial from the parent whom you charge with such an action or pattern of actions. Such actions can not only cause a parent to lose a child permanently but also lead to criminal charges.

It is important to remember that if you suspect the abuse of a child it is your duty to report the matter to authorities, regardless of your decision about seeking custody. In fact, under law it is required that an adult who knows a child is being abused come forward and report the abuse.

In a custody case, attempting to prove abuse and/or neglect can and most likely will lead to the most acrimonious of court proceedings. You will have to gather evidence and you will need to have an attorney represent your case in court. You must be absolutely certain of the truth of the charges you make before raising them in court.

No matter what, forms of abuse (physical, sexual) and/or negligence are very difficult to prove in court. This can be made less difficult, but not assured, if your grandchild's parent has been legally charged or convicted of such actions previously.

If charges of abuse and neglect are successfully proven to a court it will mean that they will likely be found unfit. Although that does not assure you will be awarded custody it greatly increases the chances.

Unstable parents.

Another factor that can be used by grandparents in a custody case is proving a child's parent unstable. This can mean financially or mental instability, which is easier to prove than abuse and neglect (though by no means a sure thing).

Financial instability must mean more than frequent job loss or change but may be proven if the child is living in destitute or impoverished conditions to the point that these conditions are not in the best interest or even harmful to the child. These include situations where the child's basic needs are not being met.

Proving mental illness is not necessarily enough to prove a parent should lose custody of their child if the evidence does not also show that there are clear threats to the safety of the child or significant red flags in the child's current environment. Again, a clear record of mental illness is a point in your favor as a grandparent seeking custody, but may not be the determining factor.

Despite parental instability, courts may still be reluctant to remove the child from their parent's care and award custody to you as the grandparent. Unstable parentage, however, in the form of physical or mental instability, does constitute grounds for a custody suit if it can be proven in court to be significant.

Parental absence.

A grandparent is most likely to be awarded custody in the case of parental absence. In the case of parental death when there is no contesting party for custody, you will be able to argue that the child needs a familial caregiver, and the courts are likely to be persuaded due to the fact that a child needs a caregiver for basic necessities such as food and shelter, as well as financial support and stability in a family situation.

You can also argue that as the grandparent you can best handle the child's other basic needs such as enrollment in school and providing school supplies and assistance, and also the child's medical care. Courts are sensitive in making sure that children have these basic necessities.

Parental absence can also be argued if the parent is imprisoned or institutionalized. Another situation where a parent can be considered absent is in the presence of a debilitating substance abuse situation.

If in either of these cases you as the grandparent are seeking custody without conflict from another contesting party, then you have a very strong chance (much stronger than in the cases of abusive, neglectful, or unstable parents) to receive custody of your grandchild from the courts.

4. What factors can be used against me in filing for custody?

Age and health.

Because courts always take into account the long-term stability of a child's situation, your age and health can be a factor in the court's decisions regarding awarding you custody.

Although people are living longer and healthier lives today than ever before, many courts still maintain a bias against older grandparents which younger grandparents may not face. At the same time, significant health problems may also cause the courts to wonder about your long-term capabilities to provide stability for your grandchild. This can be magnified in cases where multiple siblings are involved, which require even more attention and care.

Age and health may or may not be the deciding factor, so it is difficult to rule you in or out as far as how much weight is given each, but courts can take these factors into account, especially when considering the long-term care of the child. Issues regarding age and health will not necessarily make you ineligible for custody because on a case-by-case basis the court must consider the best alternative available to meet the child's needs.

Financial situation.

Due to the fact that raising a child is a somewhat expensive financial burden, a court may look at your financial situation when considering whether to award you custody of your grandchild. If you are living on a fixed income or have had financial difficulties this may be a factor the court considers, so it is important that you be sure you can take care of the child financially if you wish the court to look favorably on your suit.

Your own experience as a parent.

In a contested case where the other party seeking custody of your grandchild is your own child, your own experience as a parent is very likely to come up in court. This is because you can expect your own child to counter any charges you make against their parenting with charges that you yourself had problems raising them.

Some of these previous parenting issues could include discipline methods which, while not unconventional when your children were young, might be thought abusive by modern standards. Also any instance of neglect or instability you demonstrated in raising your own children is certainly likely to be brought up.

In some unfortunate cases, the child's parent may make up charges about you which occurred when they were young. Such charges may or may not be damaging to you in court, depending on whether there is any proof and on the parent's credibility to the judge.

Drug or alcohol use.

By the same token, it is also important to note that a history of drug or alcohol abuse by you or in your household is something that can be used against you in court. These negative things can be taken into account by the court if there is any proof of them, and sometimes the testimony of the parent can be weighed without direct proof.

Your own current relationship with your children.

You must also understand that a common defense used by parents against grandparents seeking custody of a grandchild in court involves your own current relationship with your children. A parent will often try to influence the court to believe you are retaliating against them for disagreements or rancor in your parent-child relationship by seeking custody of your grandchild.

This could mean that a grandparent with poor (or virtually) no relationship with one of their own children (especially if a contesting party) must be prepared for a judge to take that into account. These claims can be somewhat mitigated if you are claiming abuse or neglect in the case of your child when raising your grandchild, but you also have to be aware that parents will often try to "muddy the waters" by making counter-charges to lessen the impact of your claims.

Motivation for seeking custody.

A very important factor that will come up in court is your motivation for seeking custody. In a disputed case you must not appear to the judge that you are either seeking custody due to an attempt to control your own children's lives or from an overall desire to be a parent again. The best defense for you against these allegations is to remain focused on the best interest of your grandchild, and let all of your arguments for custody flow from there.

In general, since the courts (especially in states that focus mainly on parental preference) tend to side with the parents except in extreme or total absentee circumstances, you must be aware that your motives must be wholesome and your overall condition stable to be considered for custody.

However, if you are like the many other grandparents pursuing these issues because they are genuinely concerned about the welfare of their grandchildren that will reflect well on you in court.

5. Should I hire an attorney?

Although you will find more information about how to select and obtain an attorney in other sections of this book, the first question you must ask when considering filing for custody of your grandchildren is what is at stake? Once you decide on the importance of your efforts that should help you decide whether to hire an attorney.

Although there are no hard and fast rules about hiring an attorney, the following general rules will likely apply to your case if you have decided to apply for custody of your grandchild:

*If your case is going to be contested; that is, if another party has or is seeking custody (most likely one or both of your grandchild's parents) then you will likely need to hire an attorney. This is an absolute in cases where you are charging parental abuse or neglect, and likely the best decision in any case where your attempt to gain custody will be contested by a third party.

*If your case is not going to be contested; that is, in the case that the child's parent(s) are absent due to being deceased, incarcerated, or totally absent from your grandchild's life, you will need to use your best judgment as to whether to hire an attorney because one may or not be needed. Attorneys can still be extremely helpful to you even in these cases through familiarity with the system and being alert to how the state courts function where your child resides.

When you consider how many children are placed by the courts into state or foster care with those who are not familiar to them, it may pay you to ask, "What are the alternatives to my gaining custody?"

In general, in most cases where you as the grandparent are seeking custody you will want to hire an attorney to represent you in court. That does not mean an attorney will do all the work for you; it is of vital importance that you know these issues with familiarity when seeking custody and that you can aid your attorney in many ways, often lessening the financial impact on yourself.

It is also very possible that after reviewing this information you may wish to consult with an attorney before making the final decision on whether or not to apply for custody of your grandchild. Often this is the best course of action if you decide your case merits consideration for custody. Even if you ultimately decide against seeking custody, an attorney can help you with areas such as visitation or mediation.

More information on obtaining and working with an attorney can be found in the How to Hire an Attorney chapter of this book.

6. Are grandparents ever awarded custody of their grandchildren? (Yes, lots.)

Although the information included in this chapter may make it seem like an uphill battle for most grandparents seeking custody of their grandchildren (and it usually is) the fact is that grandparents are awarded custody of their grandchildren all the time.

Current estimates are that over six million children in the USA live in a grandparent's household away from their parents, and one-half of these households have no parent present.

It is taking the law a while to catch up to social norms, but today more than ever grandparents have legitimate chances to petition and potentially be awarded custody of their grandchildren. It is a difficult and often painful process, but it does happen.

4

www.caringgrandparents.com

How to Hire an Attorney

Most of us are fortunate enough to have limited experience hiring an attorney and I think we will agree that this is a good thing. In the case of this specific area of Family Law these exposures are even less frequent. So where do you start?

One good source is to ask a trusted attorney/friend who is in another field of law completely. The bar is a relatively small universe and most attorneys know how to find you the best options. Remember, choosing an attorney is not necessarily the same as choosing a friend. If you decide to hire an attorney, then this is getting serious. I have stated before that in this area of law where there is ambiguity a good and experienced attorney becomes even more important. This will become even more challenging if your grandchild(ren) live in another state.

We are continually developing and vetting sources to help grandparents and that information will be continually updated on our website at www.caringgrandparents.com.

Another source will be local grandparent support groups. If you drop a comment on our site we will try to connect you to a group close to where you live, and they may have an affiliation with a group in the city where your grandchild resides.

There are many advantages to hiring an attorney to represent you in court. Your attorney will have experience in visitation or custody laws, and in particular they will know the laws of the state your case is being tried in. A good lawyer will be very familiar with the local courts and judges, and know all the procedures as well as exactly how to present your evidence and the merits of your case.

Fair or not, your lawsuit will be taken more seriously by the courts and any other parties involved if you have an attorney representing you. Hiring a lawyer for your case signals that you are serious and that you are in court to win your rights.

Attorneys can also evaluate your case dispassionately and with a knowledge of similar cases, which can be of huge benefit to you even if they give advice against the emotions that are driving you. Courts will rule on law and not emotions and an attorney can make sure you stay on the right course in regards to the law and your chances of winning.

The decision to hire an attorney always comes down to what you are trying to accomplish. If you are filing for an uncontested visitation or guardianship agreement and things are going very smoothly you may not need a lawyer, but in a contested case an attorney is almost always a great benefit to you and most often a necessity in winning your case.

What Should You Look For in an Attorney?

For a grandparents' rights case a good attorney should be well versed on child custody issues, and have updated knowledge of family law including all the case law that relates to your suit. Far more important than your lawyer's personal charisma is his knowledge of child custody and domestic relations laws and the habits and decisions of local courts.

You are not simply seeking an attorney that agrees with you, and a lawyer who is passionate or vehement about your case is not necessarily the lawyer you want to hire. You need an attorney who can dispassionately judge the merits of your case and then base your strategy on what is most likely to succeed in court.

No attorney should make assured or overstated promises regarding child custody or visitation cases, and certainly no attorney should tell you that gaining or defending your grandparents' rights will be easy. Be wary of any lawyer who promises you an easy grandparents' rights case, and be appreciative of the attorney who levels with you and gives you a realistic assessment of your chances in court.

How Should I Find an Attorney?

Lawyers can be found through the local bar association, advertising, or personal referral. In fact, your best source for legal referral is other grandparents and grandparents' rights support groups. You might contact the clerk of court's office and ask them which lawyers they would recommend.

In all cases keep in mind the above things that you should look for in an attorney and don't be reluctant to schedule consultations with more than one lawyer. Make sure you quiz the attorney about his or her own personal experience and, in specific, his/her expertise in child custody and visitation, domestic relations, and family law before you make the decision to hire.

What Should an Attorney Do?

First of all, your lawyer should be able to answer any questions you have about the laws that will apply to your case.

Do not be afraid to ask them about anything that confuses you. They should also be able to give you a realistic appraisal of your chances in court based on similar cases they have dealt with.

An attorney should become familiar with your case and should ask you about it. You should feel free to share everything you know that might apply to your case with your lawyer, but understand that it is their responsibility to decide what is and is not important enough to be used in court.

Attorneys charge by the hour, with their rates varying according to location, their experience, the size of the firm, and the type of case. Most often they will want an upfront fee called a retainer to take your case, and that should pay for a certain amount of work before any hourly billing begins.

What Should You Do?

Your attorney must have full knowledge of your situation in order to effectively handle your case and make judgments on how to proceed.

Be frank with your attorney and do not hold information back that they will need to know due to embarrassment or because it is detrimental to you. Often your attorney can minimize such information if they are aware of it beforehand.

It is important that your attorney know everything you know about your cases. The worst surprises are those that come in court. To avoid this, give your attorney every piece of information you think pertinent to your case and let them make the call about whether or not the information is important.

Take any documents you need to your appointments with your attorney and always bring your calendar. Show up a few minutes early for your appointment. Be prepared to ask questions and bring a notebook and pen or pencil to keep notes.

5

www.caringgrandparents.com

Evidence and How to Gather It

The first step in determining what sort of evidence you will need in your visitation or custody case is to figure out what you are trying to prove. Most often, when attempting to get grandparents' rights you will have to prove to the court that not having you in the child's life is detrimental to the child's welfare. This comes directly from the Troxel case ruling.

You may also need to turn to the tactic of trying to prove that one or both of the parents are unfit parents. This is a hard task unless you have documented proof such as police reports, or reports from child protective services. Even with this the task is not easy.

These types of cases have to be handled carefully in order to keep from ripping a family apart. Because even if you win you may be doing more damage to the child than you intended. Remember that the only concern of the court is going to be what is best for the child in question.

How to Gather Evidence

Talk to family, friends, teachers, daycare staff, or anyone who has knowledge about your relationship with the child or the parent's relationship. Ask them to testify about what they know and explain why their knowledge is important.

Document everything. Keep a log of your visitations with your grandchildren and document any times you sought visitation and were denied. Keep a log of what you do when with your grandchild.

Medical and school records are good sources of proof for your granchild's residence. Remember the case must be brought in the state and court district where the child resides.

Keep track of the money you spend on the child, the places you visit with the child, and the amount of quiet at-home time you spend with the child. Make record-keeping your second job.

Photographs and videos showing you and your grand-child having fun are a fine way to establish the nature of your relationship. Remember, you want to be able to prove to the court that you are an integral part of your grandchild's life.

Write down any problems you have with the parents. Don't think that you can rely on your own testimony of acri-mony. The court will only consider specific times and events which have shown your grandchild's parents behaving irre-sponsibly or in a way that indicates they are trying to shut you out of your grandchild's life.

Keeping a photo and narrative diary of your visits with your grandchildren proves invaluable for many reasons, but if you have to convince a judge or mediator of your relationship you have the record to back up your story.

General statements will not be considered by the court—you can't simply say "They don't want me around" or "They refuse to let me visit." You must be able to point to many specific times when you have attempted regular visita-tion with your grandchild and encountered problems with the parents.

Having documentation of specific instances where you have been treated badly is the best way to establish that your rights have been ignored and is easier for a judge and a court to deal with and grasp than general statements that there are "problems."

What is hearsay?

Remember that in any court case hearsay will not be allowed. Hearsay is information someone told the witness who is testifying. Witnesses are not generally allowed to testify about something someone else told them based on hearsay rules.

What is a home study?

In some cases, you can ask for a judge to appoint someone (a third party) to do a home study of your grandchild's situation. This is usually only done in cases where abuse and/or neglect is suspected.

You can also ask a judge for psychological evaluations or drug testing of the parents in cases where there is evidence that problems exist. The strength of third-party reports can greatly enhance your chances of gaining visitation or custody rights.

What information is generally needed for a petition regarding visitation?

The procedural rules vary from state to state, but commonly when preparing a petition for visitation rights you need the following information:

1. The full legal names and addresses of the parties seeking visitation (the grandparents).

2. The full legal names, addresses, and dates of birth of the grandchildren with whom you are seeking visitation.

3. The full legal names and addresses of the parents or any other individuals with court-ordered relationships with the children.

4. The grounds that authorizes your visitation.

5. A request that the court enforce (order) the visitation.

Some states have additional requirements. If you have an attorney working for you then they will ask you this information and make the filing for you. Your case will be assigned a docket number with the court and your case will also have a case number.

The court will inform you or your attorney when your case is due to be heard. All other interested parties including the parents will be notified by the court. In many states and districts today court dockets are available online so you can check yourself to see if your case is listed.

6

What a Court Considers When Awarding Grandparents' rights

Although courts vary from state to state there are general consistencies on what courts and judges consider before awarding grandparents' rights. Generally a court considers the following factors when it decides whether or not grandparents' visitation or custody is in the best interest of the child:

The existing relationship between the grandparent and the child.

It is up to the grandparent to prove that there clearly exists a strong relationship between the child and the grandparent and that its interruption would be against the best interests of the child. This includes the documentation discussed in the previous chapter.

You will have to able to prove you play an integral role in your grandchild's life and that cutting you out of that role is against the best interest of the child. In this matter it will be invaluable if you have the written, photographic, or video evidence I alluded to in the previous chapter because in most cases the child will not testify nor should you suggest that they do.

Judges do not like to see children thrown into court, so if you have already gathered the evidence that you have been a strong and valuable part of their life it will help you immensely. Although the judge will consider your testimony on this, hard evidence goes a long way in convincing the court both of the relationship and of your resolve in gaining your grandparents' rights.

Since the burden of proof falls upon you the court will carefully consider any and all evidence you present which shows the important role you play in your grandchild's life. This is where you use the evidence-gathering strategies discussed earlier to demonstrate to the court that the existing relationship between you and your grandchild is important and vital.

The intentions of the grandparents in filing the suit.

No grandparent should go to court on a visitation or custody suit with the intent of striking back at their own children for family disagreements or conflict. You must keep in mind that the courts will look unfavorably on your suit if it appears you are only bringing the case to court in an effort to impose your will on your grandchildren's parents.

Instead you must go to the courts in good faith and convinced that having visitation or custody of your grandchildren is clearly in the best interest of the child. If you go forward with a positive attitude it will help your attorney and allow the judge to see your request in the best light.

The relationship between the child's parents or guardians and the grandparents.

The relationship you have with your own children (or the child's guardian) will be considered by the court. If the case has reached the courtroom level then the judge will expect some animosity or bad feelings between the interested parties, so that in and of itself is not necessarily going to be a reason the courts decide against you.

This is another case where negative testimony about your role in the grandchild's life can be offset if you have gathered the evidence I suggested in the previous chapter.

The time that has elapsed since the grandparents last had visitation with the child.

If it has been a long time since you last tried to visit with your grandchildren it will hurt your argument that your relationship with them is vital and important in the child's life. However, if the reason you have been unable to see your grandchild is that you have asked for and attempted visitation and been rebuffed by the child's parents, then that can actually be introduced as a point in your favor.

The arrangements already made if the parents are divorced.

Timing of agreements is important. Your best chance at having visitation rights is if they are stated in the separation agreement and that normally becomes part of the divorce decree.

If the case involves parents who are divorced, the courts will look at the divorce settlement and the custody and visitation arrangements already made. In fact, the best time to get the courts to enforce your grandparents' rights is often during a divorce when language asserting your grandparents visitation can be inserted into an agreement.

Do not be afraid to ask for this when a divorce is occurring. Often, if you are in a situation where the party with custody will end up being the party not related to you, then you can seek to include grandparents' visitation and it will be agreed to in the bargaining phase of the divorce.

Any history of abuse (physical, sexual, or emotional) or neglect on the part of the grandparent.

Gaining grandparents' visitation and/or custody becomes much harder if there is any evidence to show abuse or neglect of child (any child) on your part. Make sure you inform your lawyer of any such evidence or claims immediately before you proceed with your case so that they can assess the impact.

Any history of abuse (physical, sexual, or emotional) or neglect on the part of the parent.

Conversely, if there is any indication or evidence that the parent of the child is abusive or neglectful you will need to use that in court to prove the parent unfit. Refer to the chapter on gathering evidence to find out how to do this.

7

A General Courtroom Primer

When you go to court it is important to look and act correctly in order to get the best results for your case. Little things can matter a lot, and the way you present yourself will have an impact on how things go in court.

Get to court on time, dress and behave appropriately.

The impressions that you make on a judge are instant and important. Wear proper clothes to court. You must approach the situation with a stern, respectful resolve and avoid becoming angry or frustrated with the court process. Your appropriate appearance and respectful manner will be an asset to you when in court.

Don't panic.

There is no reason to fear going into court. You need to ask questions of your attorney when you don't understand something and there will be no need for you to be combative with the attorney for the other side. Your attorney and the judge will protect you on the stand.

Ask your attorney lots of questions when you are preparing for to go to court.

Your lawyer is familiar with the formal process of the court. Do not ask questions when you are in court unless they are very important or your lawyer has made a factual error about something important. Remain calm and keep in mind that your lawyer is the expert and you must trust him or her.

Be truthful in court.

When you testify it is imperative that you tell the truth, not only because of the risk of perjury, but because if your untruthfulness is discovered, you will look like a liar, and lying is a trait courts dislike.

Prepare yourself for testifying before the judge.

Ask your attorney to spend some time with you helping you feel comfortable with the processes and types of questions. The judge will be making a decision which will have lasting effects on your relationship with your grandchild, so being angry or disrespectful, either to the judge or to another party in front of the judge, is not wise.

Always address the judge as "Your Honor" and do not argue with the judge, the other parties, or their attorneys.

8

www.caringgrandparents.com

Best Practices: Avoiding the Courtroom

One of the best methods for maintaining full access to your grandparents' rights is to avoid the courtroom altogether. There are actions that you can take as a grandparent that will enhance your rights without resorting to litigation in the family courts.

While much of this book deals with legal and strategic approaches to your grandparents' rights I am reminded of a very wise saying: "The main thing is to keep the main thing, the main thing." The single guiding principle (The Main Thing) that we need to keep in mind is that all of what we are doing is in the best interest of the child.

Battles that happen in families and involve children can be terrible things. Try not to let emotion rule you, though, when considering the future. Remember the first rule is to do no harm. Consider carefully the impact any action on your part will have on the relationships of all the parties involved, particularly the children, before you decide to act.

It is incumbent upon us to realize two very important things when thinking about vindictiveness and hostilities: that sword cuts both ways which usually inflames and enlarges the conflict, but even more important, the grandchildren are observing the process.

I will repeat the quote of Richard S. Victor, the nationally known advocate for grandparents' rights:

"Remember, if death takes a grandparent from a grandchild, that is as tragedy, but, if petty vindictiveness and hostilities within a family amputate a grandchild from their grandparents, then that is a shame."

I am not naive in thinking that there are easy and all-encompassing methods of making things all right. There are so very many dynamics and circumstances that govern what you as a grandparent can do. I will encourage you to practice each and every best practice all the time regardless of the family situation because they will serve you well in any case.

Effective communication.

Try to focus on effective communication. Many family problems and disagreements are a result of miscommunication and misunderstandings which have damaged relationships. Healing small disagreements and trouble spots before they become full-blown breaks in the family cannot happen without effective communication.

Attempt to diffuse problems between family members by communication. This can be done through a written letter or telephone call, or a face-to-face meeting.

Avoid negativity and alienating behavior.

The legal system places a heavy weight on what is termed alienating behavior and rhetoric. So any conversations you may have about the behaviors of a wayward or erratic parent need to happen out of earshot of the children.

Remember that above all else you should not talk adversely about anyone in a child's family while in front of the child. Disparaging talk about a child's parents can come back to haunt you in many ways in a legal situation. Courts are very wary of any attempts by any party at trying to influence the children in a negative way, and judges react very strongly to such behavior.

It is important that you not engage in what is known as alienating behavior. This means an attempt to turn your grandchild against their parents or be negative toward them through your own negative statements about the situation.

Courts and judges are very sensitive to any attempts to use alienating behaviors and react strongly against it. If you are negative about the parents in front of the grandchildren it will only hurt you in court.

Be careful of what you say and to whom you say it but especially, DO NOT post anything on any Internet social media site that is in any way derogatory about either of your grandchildren's parents or their families.

On the reverse side, if you have been the victim of alienating behavior you have the right to point it out in court. Grandparents are often shut out by the parents of a child before they go to seek visitation rights. However, if this has occurred make sure you first practice good communication skills and bring this up with the children's parents before making a decision to threaten legal action.

Preventive measures.

Prevention is the best of the best practices. Whether you see trouble on the horizon in the marriage or not, be the one who offers respite care for the parents. Offer to keep the grandkids for a weekend and let the parents get away. This is a double win for you.

You will establish stronger bonds with your grandchildren and win favor with their parents for your generosity. There are many ways to insert yourself into the solution and become an ever-increasing part of your grandchildren's life. This is another of the important factors that the legal system looks for in deciding cases.

You can enlist a neutral party like a friend or member of the clergy as an informal mediator when possible.

Family counseling.

If your grandchildren's parents are willing, then family counseling may be a strong option. A trained and licensed therapist can help you work through the problems your family is experiencing in a positive way.

Mediation.

Because the adversarial nature of family court disputes can tear families apart and cause severe damage to your relationships, it is most advisable to try mediation before going to court. In fact, for many issues brought before the court you will be instructed to go to mediation by a judge in any case.

Mediation by a trusted mutual friend, pastor, or professional is infinitely better than court. Family mediation services are a low-cost way for all parties to come to agreement, typically giving a little to avoid losing a lot.

Even in many (in fact, most) cases that are filed with the court the parties are able to reach agreement, through mediation or otherwise, and the case can be settled with terms which everyone can live with. This is a positive outcome because it avoids the stigma of court-imposed decisions in regards to your grandchildren.

Grandparents' Guardianship

Some states allow grandparents' guardianship, which is a category between grandparents' visitation and grandparents' custody. Guardianship has the same effect as providing parental authority to a grandparent (or in some cases another third party). Generally, guardianship is less permanent than custody. Guardianship is very effective in the cases of military deployment.

What is guardianship?

Guardianship is a way for grandparents to take legal responsibility for their grandchild based on the previous relationship that they have established with the child. It is not necessary to be related to a child to gain guardianship, but it is necessary to have a significant bond and relationship, and grandparents most often have that bond.

Grandparents are also ideal for guardianship because the children are allowed to stay in the family they are familiar with. Guardianship is like custody in the fact that once it is established, it can only be changed by agreement between the parties or by order of the court.

How does the court come to a decision on guardianship?

As always, when determining guardianship, the court looks to the best interest of the child. In some instances of guardianship, the parent with custody of the child leaves the child with a relative or grandparent indefinitely. The relative or third party is thus left responsible for the child and cannot attain required authority to take care for the child.

As a result, the relative or third party will often seek guardianship of the child, so he or she can make important legal, medical, and educational decisions for the child while the parent is away and in the best interest of the child.

In other instances, the parent with custody may leave the child with the relative or third party while the parent is unable to care for the child temporarily, such as a parent who is incarcerated, in a rehabilitation facility, or otherwise absent.

In those instances, the relative or third party may seek temporary guardianship of the child. Temporary guardianship allows for the relative or third party to make important legal, medical, and educational decisions on behalf of the child while the parent is unable to care for the child.

What is the difference between custody and guardianship?

Guardianship is often more temporary than custody. The court can thus revoke guardianship if the biological parent of the child returns. The courts are reluctant to revoke parental rights unless the parent is unfit or has shown a history of abuse and neglect toward the child.

The Case for Grandparents' rights

Situations in which grandparents raise their grandchildren are certainly not new, but the cases of this happening have been skyrocketing over the last decade. Studies are long overdue as to the number of grandparents in the country who are raising their grandchildren. State and federal government agencies that are responsible for gathering such family data need to address this issue.

The Reality Today

The number of grandparents raising their grandchildren has rapidly increased. With this increase some grandparents are finding themselves overwhelmed. Wholeheartedly they take on the task of providing a loving, safe, stable environment for their grandchildren to thrive and grown within. Without regard to their own financial status, physical health or personal needs, grandparents are undertaking being a parent to their grandchildren, with very few given legal rights to do so.

Circumstances surrounding grandchildren being raised by their grandparents vary tremendously. The best scenario is where the biological parents have a working relationship with the grandparents, thus allowing them to work jointly in the best interest of the children.

However, this is not the situation for the vast majority of grandchildren being raised by grandparents. These grandchildren are products of dysfunctional parents, drug-addicted parents, neglectful parents, abusive parents, extremely violent environments, non-supervisory parents, and incarcerated parents.

Grandparents and Divorce

When a divorce takes place in the family, each person is affected differently. The separation of the family unit affects everyone. There is blame and hurt from everyone in the family and it is never an easy time for anyone to have to go through.

When the parents separate and/or divorce, it affects the grandparents' rights when it comes to visitation with the grandchildren. With the divorce rate hovering at 50 percent, there is a one in two chance this scenario will come up for the grandparents to deal with. When it comes to custody issues the grandparents are very concerned about what will happen to their grandchildren.

The grandparents must be able to have a continued relationship with their grandchildren. This will let the grandkids have some normalcy in their lives like they had before. Grandparents love their grandchildren, and anything that they can do to help during this time is of great value to the parents and the children.

The parents should not make the children pay for what has happened to their relationship. I refer to this punishing behavior as beating each other over the head with the children. and/or the grandparents It is also imperative that the grandparents refrain from taking sides no matter how hard that may be. Not only is this damaging to the children, but it can and will be used against the grandparents if this issue goes to mediation or the courts.

Just because there is anger between the parents does not mean that the grandparents have to be shut out of their grandchildren's lives. This is referred to in the court proceedings as alienating behavior (see the chapter on avoiding the courtroom). Once again the grandparents have to be careful not to get caught up in this also.

The parents should think about what this can do to the children and know the effect of the children being deprived of a good relationship with their grandparents. The only thing that holding your children back from their grandparents does is to make your children suffer.

Caring grandparents love to spoil their grandchildren and have special feelings for them. In some cases, grandparents are unable to have a close relationship with their grandchildren because of health issues and other reasons, but this does not mean that the grandparents don't love or want to see their grandchildren, and this is something that the parents must think about.

When a couple divorces they must decide, or let the court decide, which parent the children will live with and in most cases, there is shared custody of the children. This makes it easier for the parents both being with their children to allow the children to visit their grandparents.

When the parents of a child divorce and the grandparents have the possibility of losing their rights to see their grandchildren, steps need to be taken to assure that there is an ongoing relationship between them and their grandchildren. Grandparents should be there during a divorce not only to give the parents support but also for the children.

This is important for the grandparents to have access to being with their grandchildren. There are certain cases when abuse is involved, and this is especially when the grandparents should do everything in their power to be there to make sure that they have close ongoing access to their grandchildren, create a sense of security, and provide a feeling of continuity.

Grandparents should have visitation rights with grandchildren in most cases. After all, grandparents are some of the closest people in their lives and can bring security, love, and the feeling of being safe to their grandchildren.

All children deserve to have a close bond with their family members. Just because there is a divorce, the parents should not hold that against other family members. They need to think about their children and what is best for them, which is being with the ones that they love and people who care for them. Visitation rights for grandparents are very important for families to be able to stay together no matter what the situation.

The grandparents can be of big help to the parents. They can help take care of the children while the parents are trying to move on with their lives. The parents will want to try to keep their children's lives as uncomplicated as possible during this difficult time. The grandparents can be there for the children if something bad should happen to the parents, and that is enough of a reason to always allow the grandparents to see their grandchildren.

The Case for Grandparents' rights

By not maintaining adequate laws to protect our children, our legal system has miserably failed them. The antiquated laws governing grandparents' rights need to be revised to reflect the times we live in. More and more children's childhoods will be destroyed, leaving them to become part of the juvenile justice system or suffer at the hands of their parents or unfit guardians.

If the laws do not change allowing grandparents legal rights to protect and defend their grandchildren they will just become statistics society will have to contend with. Just another thing our state and federal legal system should have and could have prevented, but refused and failed to do so.

11

Caring Grandparents: Additional Best Practices

Here are some additional best practices I have gathered that you might want to focus on in your relationship with your grandchild.

Discipline techniques

Grandparents who find themselves having custody of their grandchildren, or just spending a great deal of time with them during visitation, may wonder about discipline techniques. Whenever possible get the parents' input and be supportive and consistent with their discipline practices.

One effective technique used often today is the time-out. Children who are used to "time-outs" may stump grandparents raised many years ago in entirely different circumstances.

Time-outs can effectively stop behaviors that are especially hard to discipline. A time-out can also serve as disciplinary action for a particularly aggressive or impulsive grandkid! These discipline problems can include everything from a temper tantrum to cursing to name-calling to spitting to acting up to biting.

If your grandchild is very angry or actually having a tantrum, time-outs can be a very effective form of discipline. They are a "stop" behavior discipline rather than a "start" behavior discipline. They also serve to save your sanity from time to time.

Start the time-out before you lose your temper. It adds effectiveness to your discipline since the child has more confidence in your consistency.

It is best if all adults and older siblings follow the same rules to use this form of discipline. This includes parents, grandparents, and caregivers.

Time-out discipline tips include:

1. Don't bargain, discuss, or argue with children.

2. Use one minute of time-out for each year of age.

3. Ignore all yelling, sarcastic remarks, and screaming while time-out proceeds. You must even ignore cursing.

4. Use a timer. Set the timer only when the child is quiet; i.e., not screaming, cursing, banging around, or using disrespectful language.

5. After the time-out is over, open the door and permit the child to leave. There should be no further explanation, warning, or apology.

Grandparents and adoption.

One of the greatest of experiences in life is becoming a grandparent, even if it comes through unconventional means.

Grandparents whose children adopt have a wonderful chance to welcome a brand new person into their family.

As with all major life changes, adoption is both a wonderful and challenging experience, filled with excitement, adjustment, and joy. This is no less true for the grandparents, as they watch their own beloved children dealing with all the emotions that come with adopting a child.

Adoption is becoming more frequent in our society and should be embraced by grandparents as they find this new life added to the family.

Here are some tips to consider if you are becoming a grandparent through adoption:

1. Be a partner in parenting, taking your cues from the parent and respecting that the parent is in charge. While you certainly can share your wisdom and experience, remember that your son or daughter will need to find their own way—just as you did when you were a new parent.

2. People are fascinated by adoption, and this fascination can lead well-meaning friends and neighbors to pose very personal questions. Remember that a child's adoption story is akin to a conception story. It is private, and one should consult with the adopted person before sharing the details.

3. If a grandchild is coming from another country, grandparents can research the culture and history of that country and pass along information to their adult child. Your adult child will appreciate the enthusiasm!

4. Avoid trying to steer your adult children in any way. Support their decisions and let them know that you will love your grandchild unconditionally.

5. Don't give advice when it isn't asked for. Let your adult children experience the process and don't bring up every negative story that you've seen on TV or in a movie.

6. Remember, throughout, that your grandchildren are connected to you and to the family. They may not look a lot like you or your child, but they will develop similar voice patterns, talents, tastes, and interests.

12

The Troxell Decision

"There are times when we find Logic and Law to be strange bedfellows."

Neil Taft

I debated about including this document in the book, but since it is the single most significant document that colors all legal proceedings surround **Grandparents' Rights** and the fate of our grandchildren, I determined it was necessary. I won't kid you about how arduous it is to read court briefs in general, much less one that has gone to the Supreme Court.

You really don't have to be an attorney to understand the majority of this ruling. One of my main reasons for including this is that these nine Justices decided the fate of grandparents and grandchildren for many years to come, and there was nothing near to unanimity in their reasoning. There are two ways to look at this; one is that it is terrible and the other is that since most family court decisions are not challenged in the Supreme Court, and it is known that the right judge will rule in a pretty predictable way…well, it might just be against the law for me to finish that sentence.

As things stand, the Troxell decision is the standard by which grandparents' rights are currently measured in the courts.

TROXEL et vir. v. GRANVILLE

certiorari to the supreme court of Washington

No. 99-138. Argued January 12, 2000--Decided June 5, 2000

Washington Rev. Code §26.10.160(3) permits "[a]ny person" to petition for visitation rights "at any time" and authorizes state superior courts to grant such rights whenever visitation may serve a child's best interest. Petitioners Troxel petitioned for the right to visit their deceased son's daughters. Respondent Granville, the girls' mother, did not oppose all visitation, but objected to the amount sought by the Troxels. The Superior Court ordered more visitation than Granville desired, and she appealed. The State Court of Appeals reversed and dismissed the Troxels' petition. In affirming, the State Supreme Court held, inter alia, that §26.10.160(3) unconstitutionally infringes on parents' fundamental right to rear their children. Reasoning that the Federal Constitution permits a State to interfere with this right only to prevent harm or potential harm to the child, it found that §26.10.160(3) does not require a threshold showing of harm and sweeps too broadly by permitting any person to petition at any time with the only requirement being that the visitation serve the best interest of the child.

Held: The judgment is affirmed.

137 Wash. 2d 1, 969 P. 2d 21, affirmed.

Justice O'Connor, joined by The Chief Justice, Justice Ginsburg, and Justice Breyer, concluded that §26.10.160(3), as applied to Granville and her family, violates her due process right to make decisions concerning the care, custody, and control of her daughters. Pp. 5-17.

(a) The Fourteenth Amendment's Due Process Clause has a substantive component that "provides heightened protection against government interference with certain fundamental rights and liberty interests," Washington v. Glucksberg, 521 U. S. 702, 720, including parents' fundamental right to make decisions concerning the care, custody, and control of their children, see, e.g., Stanley v. Illinois, 405 U. S. 645, 651. Pp. 5-8.

(b) Washington's breathtakingly broad statute effectively permits a court to disregard and overturn any decision by a fit custodial parent concerning visitation whenever a third party affected by the decision files a visitation petition, based solely on the judge's determination of the child's best interest. A parent's estimation of the child's best interest is accorded no deference. The State Supreme Court had the opportunity, but declined, to give §26.10.160(3) a narrower reading. A combination of several factors compels the conclusion that §26.10.160(3), as applied here, exceeded the bounds of the Due Process Clause. First, the Troxels did not allege, and no court has found, that Granville was an unfit parent. There is a presumption that fit parents act in their children's best interests, Parham v. J. R., 442 U. S. 584, 602; there is normally no reason for the State to inject itself into the private realm of the family to further question fit parents' ability to make the best decisions regarding their children, see, e.g., Reno v. Flores, 507 U. S. 292, 304. The problem here is not that the Superior Court intervened, but that when it did so, it gave no special

67

weight to Granville's determination of her daughters' best interests. More importantly, that court appears to have applied the opposite presumption, favoring grandparent visitation. In effect, it placed on Granville the burden of disproving that visitation would be in her daughters' best interest and thus failed to provide any protection for her fundamental right. The court also gave no weight to Granville's having assented to visitation even before the filing of the petition or subsequent court intervention. These factors, when considered with the Superior Court's slender findings, show that this case involves nothing more than a simple disagreement between the court and Granville concerning her children's best interests, and that the visitation order was an unconstitutional infringement on Granville's right to make decisions regarding the rearing of her children. Pp. 8-14.

(c) Because the instant decision rests on §26.10.160(3)'s sweeping breadth and its application here, there is no need to consider the question whether the Due Process Clause requires all nonparental visitation statutes to include a showing of harm or potential harm to the child as a condition precedent to granting visitation or to decide the precise scope of the parental due process right in the visitation context. There is also no reason to remand this case for further proceedings. The visitation order clearly violated the Constitution, and the parties should not be forced into additional litigation that would further burden Granville's parental right. Pp. 14-17.

Justice Souter concluded that the Washington Supreme Court's second reason for invalidating its own state statute—that it sweeps too broadly in authorizing any person at any time to request (and a judge to award) visitation rights, subject only to the State's particular best-interests standard—is consistent with this Court's prior cases. This ends the case, and there is no need to decide whether harm is required or to consider the precise scope of a parent's right or its necessary protections. Pp. 1-5.

Justice Thomas agreed that this Court's recognition of a fundamental right of parents to direct their children's upbringing resolves this case, but concluded that strict scrutiny is the appropriate standard of review to apply to infringements of fundamental rights. Here, the State lacks a compelling interest in second-guessing a fit parent's decision regarding visitation with third parties. Pp. 1-2.

O'Connor, J., announced the judgment of the Court and delivered an opinion, in which Rehnquist, C. J., and Ginsburg and Breyer, JJ., joined. Souter, J., and Thomas, J., filed opinions concurring in the judgment. Stevens, J., Scalia, J., and Kennedy, J., filed dissenting opinions.

JENIFER TROXEL, et vir, PETITIONERS v.
TOMMIE GRANVILLE
on writ of certiorari to the supreme court
of Washington
[June 5, 2000]

Section 26.10.160(3) of the Revised Code of Washington permits "[a]ny person" to petition a superior court for visitation rights "at any time," and authorizes that court to grant such visitation rights whenever "visitation may serve the best interest of the child." Petitioners Jenifer and Gary Troxel petitioned a Washington Superior Court for the right to visit their grandchildren, Isabelle and Natalie Troxel. Respondent Tommie Granville, the mother of Isabelle and Natalie, opposed the petition. The case ultimately reached the Washington Supreme Court, which held that §26.10.160(3) unconstitutionally interferes with the fundamental right of parents to rear their children.

I

Tommie Granville and Brad Troxel shared a relationship that ended in June 1991. The two never married, but they had two daughters, Isabelle and Natalie. Jenifer and Gary Troxel are Brad's parents, and thus the paternal grandparents of Isabelle and Natalie. After Tommie and Brad separated in 1991, Brad lived with his parents and regularly brought his daughters to his parents' home for weekend visitation. Brad committed suicide in May 1993. Although the Troxels at first continued to see Isabelle and Natalie on a regular basis after their son's death, Tommie Granville informed the Troxels in October 1993 that she wished to limit their visitation with her daughters to one short visit per month. In re Smith, 137 Wash. 2d 1, 6, 969 P. 2d 21, 23-24 (1998); In re Troxel, 87 Wash. App. 131, 133, 940 P. 2d 698, 698-699 (1997).

In December 1993, the Troxels commenced the present action by filing, in the Washington Superior Court for Skagit County, a petition to obtain visitation rights with Isabelle and Natalie. The Troxels filed their petition under two Washington statutes, Wash. Rev. Code §§26.09.240 and 26.10.160(3) (1994). Only the latter statute is at issue in this case. Section 26.10.160(3) provides: "Any person may petition the court for visitation rights at any time including, but not limited to, custody proceedings. The court may order visitation rights for any person when visitation may serve the best interest of the child whether or not there has been any change of circumstances." At trial, the Troxels requested two weekends of overnight visitation per month and two weeks of visitation each summer. Granville did not oppose visitation altogether, but instead asked the court to order one day of visitation per month with no overnight stay. 87 Wash. App., at 133-134, 940

P. 2d, at 699. In 1995, the Superior Court issued an oral ruling and entered a visitation decree ordering visitation one weekend per month, one week during the summer, and four hours on both of the petitioning grandparents' birthdays. 137 Wash. 2d, at 6, 969 P. 2d, at 23; App. to Pet. for Cert. 76a-78a.

Granville appealed, during which time she married Kelly Wynn. Before addressing the merits of Granville's appeal, the Washington Court of Appeals remanded the case to the Superior Court for entry of written findings of fact and conclusions of law. 137 Wash.2d, at 6, 969 P. 2d, at 23. On remand, the Superior Court found that visitation was in Isabelle and Natalie's best interests:

"The Petitioners [the Troxels] are part of a large, central, loving family, all located in this area, and the Petitioners can provide opportunities for the children in the areas of cousins and music.

" ... The court took into consideration all factors regarding the best interest of the children and considered all the testimony before it. The children would be benefitted from spending quality time with the Petitioners, provided that that time is balanced with time with the childrens' [sic] nuclear family. The court finds that the childrens' [sic] best interests are served by spending time with their mother and stepfather's other six children." App. 70a.

Approximately nine months after the Superior Court entered its order on remand, Granville's husband formally adopted Isabelle and Natalie. Id., at 60a-67a.

The Washington Court of Appeals reversed the lower court's visitation order and dismissed the Troxels' petition for visitation, holding that nonparents lack standing to seek visitation under §26.10.160(3) unless a custody action is pending. In the Court of Appeals' view, that limitation on nonparental visitation actions was "consistent with the constitutional restrictions on state interference with parents' fundamental liberty interest in the care, custody, and management of their children." 87 Wash. App., at 135, 940 P. 2d, at 700 (internal quotation marks omitted). Having resolved the case on the statutory ground, however, the Court of Appeals did not expressly pass on Granville's constitutional challenge to the visitation statute. Id., at 138, 940 P. 2d, at 701.

The Washington Supreme Court granted the Troxels' petition for review and, after consolidating their case with two other visitation cases, affirmed. The court disagreed with the Court of Appeals' decision on the statutory issue and found that the plain language of §26.10.160(3) gave the Troxels standing to seek visitation, irrespective of whether a custody action was pending. 137 Wash. 2d, at 12, 969 P. 2d, at 26-27. The Washington Supreme Court nevertheless agreed with the Court of Appeals' ultimate conclusion that the Troxels could not obtain visitation of Isabelle and Natalie pursuant to §26.10.160(3). The court rested its decision on the Federal Constitution, holding that §26.10.160(3) unconstitutionally infringes on the fundamental right of parents to rear their children. In the court's view, there were at least two problems with the nonparental visitation statute. First, according to the Washington Supreme Court, the Constitution permits a State to interfere with the right of parents to rear their children only to prevent harm or potential harm to a child. Section 26.10.160(3) fails that standard because it requires no threshold showing of harm. Id., at 15-20, 969 P. 2d, at 28-30. Second, by allowing "'any person' to petition for forced visitation of a child at 'any time' with the only requirement being that the visitation serve the best interest of the child," the Washington visitation statute sweeps too broadly. Id., at 20, 969 P. 2d, at 30. "It is not within the province of the state to make significant decisions concerning the custody of children merely because it could make a 'better' decision." Ibid., 969 P. 2d, at 31. The Washington Supreme Court held that "[p]arents have a right to limit visitation of their children with third persons," and that between parents and judges, "the parents should be the ones to choose whether to expose their children to certain people or ideas." Id., at 21, 969 P. 2d, at 31. Four justices dissented from the Washington Supreme Court's holding on the constitutionality of the statute. Id., at 23-43, 969 P. 2d, at 32-42.

We granted certiorari, 527 U. S. 1069 (1999), and now affirm the judgment.

II

The demographic changes of the past century make it difficult to speak of an average American family. The composition of families varies greatly from household to household. While many children may have two married parents and grandparents who visit regularly, many other children are raised in single-parent households. In 1996, children living with only one parent accounted for 28 percent of all children under age 18 in the United States. U. S. Dept. of Commerce, Bureau of Census, Current Population Reports, 1997 Population Profile of the United States 27 (1998). Understandably, in these single-parent households, persons outside the nuclear family are called upon with increasing frequency to assist in the everyday tasks of child rearing. In many cases, grandparents play an important role. For example, in 1998, approximately 4 million children—or 5.6 percent of all children under age 18— lived in the household of their grandparents. U. S. Dept. of Commerce, Bureau of Census, Current Population Reports, Marital Status and Living Arrangements: March 1998 (Update), p. i (1998).

The nationwide enactment of nonparental visitation statutes is assuredly due, in some part, to the States' recognition of these changing realities of the American family. Because grandparents and other relatives undertake duties of a parental nature in many households, States have sought to ensure the welfare of the children therein by protecting the relationships those children form with such third parties. The States' nonparental visitation statutes are further supported by a recognition, which varies from State to State, that children should have the opportunity to benefit from relationships with statutorily specified persons—for example, their grandparents. The extension of statutory rights in this area to persons other than a child's parents, however, comes with an obvious cost. For example, the State's recognition of an independent third-party interest in a child can place a substantial burden on the traditional parent-child relationship. Contrary to Justice Stevens' accusation, our description of state nonparental visitation statutes in these terms, of course, is not meant to suggest that "children are so much chattel." Post, at 10 (dissenting opinion). Rather, our terminology is intended to highlight the fact that these statutes can present questions of constitutional import. In this case, we are presented with just such a question. Specifically, we are asked to decide whether §26.10.160(3), as applied to Tommie Granville and her family, violates the Federal Constitution.

The Fourteenth Amendment provides that no State shall "deprive any person of life, liberty, or property, without due process of law." We have long recognized that the Amendment's Due Process Clause, like its Fifth Amendment counterpart, "guarantees more than fair process." Washington v. Glucksberg, 521 U. S. 702, 719 (1997). The Clause also includes a substantive component that "provides heightened protection against government interference with certain fundamental rights and liberty interests." Id., at 720; see also Reno v. Flores, 507 U. S. 292, 301-302 (1993).

The liberty interest at issue in this case—the interest of parents in the care, custody, and control of their children—is perhaps the oldest of the fundamental liberty interests recognized by this Court. More than 75 years ago, in Meyer v. Nebraska, 262 U. S. 390, 399, 401 (1923), we held that the "liberty" protected by the Due Process Clause includes the right of parents to "establish a home and bring up children" and "to control the education of their own." Two years later, in Pierce v. Society of Sisters, 268 U. S. 510, 534-535 (1925), we again held that the "liberty of parents and guardians" includes the right "to direct the upbringing and education of children under their control." We explained in Pierce that "[t]he child is not the mere creature of the State; those who nurture him and direct his destiny have the right, coupled with the high duty, to recognize and prepare him for additional obligations." Id., at 535. We returned to the subject in Prince v. Massachusetts, 321 U. S. 158 (1944), and again confirmed that there is a constitutional dimension to the right of parents to direct the upbringing of their children. "It is cardinal with us that the custody, care and nurture of the child reside first in the parents, whose primary function and freedom include preparation for obligations the state can neither supply nor hinder." Id., at 166.

In subsequent cases also, we have recognized the fundamental right of parents to make decisions concerning the care, custody, and control of their children. See, e.g., Stanley v. Illinois, 405 U. S. 645, 651 (1972) ("It is plain that the interest of a parent in the companionship, care, custody, and management of his or her children 'come[s] to this Court with a momentum for respect lacking when appeal is made to liberties which derive merely from shifting economic arrangements'" (citation omitted)); Wisconsin v. Yoder, 406 U. S. 205, 232 (1972) ("The history and culture of Western civilization reflect a strong tradition of parental concern for the nurture and upbringing of their children. This primary role of the parents in the upbringing of their children is now established beyond debate as an enduring American tradition"); Quilloin v. Walcott, 434 U. S. 246, 255 (1978) ("We have recognized on numerous occasions that the relationship between parent and child is constitutionally protected"); Parham v. J. R., 442 U. S. 584, 602 (1979) ("Our jurisprudence historically has reflected Western civilization concepts of the family as a unit with broad parental authority over minor children. Our cases have consistently followed that course"); Santosky v. Kramer, 455 U. S. 745, 753 (1982) (discussing "[t]he fundamental liberty interest of natural parents in the care, custody, and management of their child"); Glucksberg, supra, at 720 ("In a long line of cases, we have held that, in addition to the specific freedoms protected by the Bill of Rights, the 'liberty' specially protected by the Due Process Clause includes the righ[t]...to direct the education and upbringing of one's children" (citing Meyer and Pierce)). In light of this extensive precedent, it cannot now be doubted that the Due Process Clause of the Fourteenth Amendment protects the fundamental right of parents to make decisions concerning the care, custody, and control of their children.

Section 26.10.160(3), as applied to Granville and her family in this case, unconstitutionally infringes on that fundamental parental right. The Washington nonparental visitation statute is breathtakingly broad. According to the statute's text, "[a]ny person may petition the court for visitation rights at any time," and the court may grant such visitation rights whenever "visitation may serve the best interest of the child." §26.10.160(3) (emphases added). That language effectively permits any third party seeking visitation to subject any decision by a parent concerning visitation of the parent's children to state-court review. Once the visitation petition has been filed in court and the matter is placed before a judge, a parent's decision that visitation would not be in the child's best interest is accorded no deference. Section 26.10.160(3) contains no requirement that a court accord the parent's decision any presumption of validity or any weight whatsoever. Instead, the Washington statute places the best-interest determination solely in the hands of the judge. Should the judge disagree with the parent's estimation of the child's best interests, the judge's view necessarily prevails. Thus, in practical effect, in the State of Washington a court can disregard and overturn any decision by a fit custodial parent concerning visitation whenever a third party affected by the decision files a visitation petition, based solely on the judge's determination of the child's best interests. The Washington Supreme Court had the opportunity to give §26.10.160(3) a narrower reading, but it declined to do so. See, e.g., 137 Wash. 2d, at 5, 969 P. 2d, at 23 ("[The statute] allow[s] any person, at any time, to petition for visitation without regard to relationship to the child, without regard to changed circumstances, and without regard to harm"); id., at 20, 969 P. 2d, at 30 ("[The statute] allow[s] 'any person' to petition for forced visitation of a child at 'any time' with the only requirement being that the visitation serve the best interest of the child").

Turning to the facts of this case, the record reveals that the Superior Court's order was based on precisely the type of mere disagreement we have just described and nothing more. The Superior Court's order was not founded on any special factors that might justify the State's interference with Granville's fundamental right to make decisions concerning the rearing of her two daughters. To be sure, this case involves a visitation petition filed by grandparents soon after the death of their son—the father of Isabelle and Natalie—but the combination of several factors here compels our conclusion that §26.10.160(3), as applied, exceeded the bounds of the Due Process Clause.

First, the Troxels did not allege, and no court has found, that Granville was an unfit parent. That aspect of the case is important, for there is a presumption that fit parents act in the best interests of their children. As this Court explained in Parham:

"[O]ur constitutional system long ago rejected any notion that a child is the mere creature of the State and, on the contrary, asserted that parents generally have the right, coupled with the high duty, to recognize and prepare [their children] for additional obligations. ...The law's concept of the family rests on a presumption that parents possess what a child lacks in maturity, experience, and capacity for judgment required for making life's difficult decisions. More important, historically it has recognized that natural bonds of affection lead parents to act in the best interests of their children." 442 U. S., at 602 (alteration in original) (internal quotation marks and citations omitted).

Accordingly, so long as a parent adequately cares for his or her children (i.e., is fit), there will normally be no reason for the State to inject itself into the private realm of the family to further question the ability of that parent to make the best decisions concerning the rearing of that parent's children. See, e.g., Flores, 507 U. S., at 304.

The problem here is not that the Washington Superior Court intervened, but that when it did so, it gave no special weight at all to Granville's determination of her daughters' best interests. More importantly, it appears that the Superior Court applied exactly the opposite presumption. In reciting its oral ruling after the conclusion of closing arguments, the Superior Court judge explained:

"The burden is to show that it is in the best interest of the children to have some visitation and some quality time with their grandparents. I think in most situations a commonsensical approach [is that] it is normally in the best interest of the children to spend quality time with the grandparent, unless the grandparent, [sic] there are some issues or problems involved wherein the grandparents, their lifestyles are going to impact adversely upon the children. That certainly isn't the case here from what I can tell." Verbatim Report of Proceedings in In re Troxel, No. 93-3-00650-7 (Wash. Super. Ct., Dec. 14, 19, 1994), p. 213 (hereinafter Verbatim Report).

The judge's comments suggest that he presumed the grandparents' request should be granted unless the children would be "impact[ed] adversely." In effect, the judge placed on Granville, the fit custodial parent, the burden of disproving that visitation would be in the best interest of her daughters. The judge reiterated moments later: "I think [visitation with the Troxels] would be in the best interest of the children and I haven't been shown it is not in [the] best interest of the children." Id., at 214.

The decisional framework employed by the Superior Court directly contravened the traditional presumption that a fit parent will act in the best interest of his or her child. See Parham, supra, at 602. In that respect, the court's presumption failed to provide any protection for Granville's fundamental constitutional right to make decisions concerning the rearing of her own daughters. Cf., e.g., Cal. Fam. Code Ann. §3104(e) (West 1994) (rebuttable presumption that grandparent visitation is not in child's best interest if parents agree that visitation rights should not be granted); Me. Rev. Stat. Ann., Tit. 19A, §1803(3) (1998) (court may award grandparent visitation if in best interest of child and "would not significantly interfere with any parent-child relationship or with the parent's rightful authority over the child"); Minn. Stat. §257.022(2)(a)(2) (1998) (court may award grandparent visitation if in best interest of child and "such visitation would not interfere with the parent-child relationship"); Neb. Rev. Stat. §43-1802(2) (1998) (court must find "by clear and convincing evidence" that grandparent visitation "will not adversely interfere with the parent-child relationship"); R. I. Gen. Laws §15-5-24.3(a)(2)(v) (Supp. 1999) (grandparent must rebut, by clear and convincing evidence, presumption that parent's decision to refuse grandparent visitation was reasonable); Utah Code Ann. §30-5-2(2)(e) (1998) (same); Hoff v. Berg, 595 N. W. 2d 285, 291-292 (N. D. 1999) (holding North Dakota grandparent visitation statute unconstitutional because State has no "compelling interest in presuming visitation rights of grandparents to an unmarried minor are in the child's best interests and forcing parents to accede to court-ordered grandparental visitation unless the parents are first able to prove such visitation is not in the best interests of their minor child"). In an ideal world, parents might always seek to cultivate the bonds between grandparents and their grandchildren. Needless to say, however, our world is far from perfect, and in it the decision whether such an intergenerational relationship would be beneficial in any specific case is for the parent to make in the first instance. And, if a fit parent's decision of the kind at issue here becomes subject to judicial review, the court must accord at least some special weight to the parent's own determination.

Finally, we note that there is no allegation that Granville ever sought to cut off visitation entirely. Rather, the present dispute originated when Granville informed the Troxels that she would prefer to restrict their visitation with Isabelle and Natalie to one short visit per month and special holidays. See 87 Wash. App., at 133, 940 P. 2d, at 699; Verbatim Report 12. In the Superior Court proceedings Granville did not oppose visitation but instead asked that the duration of any visitation order be shorter than that requested by the Troxels. While the Troxels requested two weekends per month and two full weeks in the summer, Granville asked the Superior Court to order only one day of visitation per month (with no overnight stay) and participation in the Granville family's holiday celebrations. See 87 Wash. App., at 133, 940 P. 2d, at 699; Verbatim Report 9 ("Right off the bat we'd like to say that our position is that grandparent visitation is in the best interest of the children. It is a matter of how much and how it is going to be structured") (opening statement by Granville's attorney). The Superior Court gave no weight to Granville's having assented to visitation even before the filing of any visitation petition or subsequent court intervention. The court instead rejected Granville's proposal and settled on a middle ground, ordering one weekend of visitation per month, one week in the summer, and time on both of the petitioning grandparents' birthdays. See 87 Wash. App., at 133-134, 940 P. 2d, at 699; Verbatim Report 216-221. Significantly, many other States expressly provide by statute that courts may not award visitation unless a parent has denied (or unreasonably denied) visitation to the concerned third party. See, e.g., Miss. Code Ann. §93-16-3(2)(a) (1994) (court must find that "the parent or custodian of the child unreasonably denied the grandparent visitation rights with the child"); Ore. Rev. Stat. §109.121(1)(a)(B) (1997) (court may award visitation if the "custodian of the child has denied the grandparent reasonable opportunity to visit the child"); R. I. Gen. Laws §15-5-24.3(a)(2)(iii)-(iv) (Supp. 1999) (court must find that parents prevented grandparent from visiting grandchild and that "there is no other way the petitioner is able to visit his or her grandchild without court intervention").

81

Considered together with the Superior Court's reasons for awarding visitation to the Troxels, the combination of these factors demonstrates that the visitation order in this case was an unconstitutional infringement on Granville's fundamental right to make decisions concerning the care, custody, and control of her two daughters. The Washington Superior Court failed to accord the determination of Granville, a fit custodial parent, any material weight. In fact, the Superior Court made only two formal findings in support of its visitation order. First, the Troxels "are part of a large, central, loving family, all located in this area, and the [Troxels] can provide opportunities for the children in the areas of cousins and music." App. 70a. Second, "[t]he children would be benefitted from spending quality time with the [Troxels], provided that that time is balanced with time with the childrens' [sic] nuclear family." Ibid. These slender findings, in combination with the court's announced presumption in favor of grandparent visitation and its failure to accord significant weight to Granville's already having offered meaningful visitation to the Troxels, show that this case involves nothing more than a simple disagreement between the Washington Superior Court and Granville concerning her children's best interests. The Superior Court's announced reason for ordering one week of visitation in the summer demonstrates our conclusion well: "I look back on some personal experiences.... We always spen[t] as kids a week with one set of grandparents and another set of grandparents, [and] it happened to work out in our family that [it] turned out to be an enjoyable experience. Maybe that can, in this family, if that is how it works out." Verbatim Report 220-221. As we have explained, the Due Process Clause does not permit a State to infringe on the fundamental right of parents to make childrearing decisions simply because a state judge believes a "better" decision could be made. Neither the

82

Washington nonparental visitation statute generally—which places no limits on either the persons who may petition for visitation or the circumstances in which such a petition may be granted—nor the Superior Court in this specific case required anything more. Accordingly, we hold that §26.10.160(3), as applied in this case, is unconstitutional.

Because we rest our decision on the sweeping breadth of §26.10.160(3) and the application of that broad, unlimited power in this case, we do not consider the primary constitutional question passed on by the Washington Supreme Court—whether the Due Process Clause requires all nonparental visitation statutes to include a showing of harm or potential harm to the child as a condition precedent to granting visitation. We do not, and need not, define today the precise scope of the parental due process right in the visitation context. In this respect, we agree with Justice Kennedy that the constitutionality of any standard for awarding visitation turns on the specific manner in which that standard is applied and that the constitutional protections in this area are best "elaborated with care." Post, at 9 (dissenting opinion). Because much state-court adjudication in this context occurs on a case-by-case basis, we would be hesitant to hold that specific nonparental visitation statutes violate the Due Process Clause as a per se matter.1 See, e.g., Fairbanks v. McCarter, 330 Md. 39, 49-50, 622 A. 2d 121, 126-127 (1993) (interpreting best-interest standard in grandparent visitation statute normally to require court's consideration of certain factors); Williams v. Williams, 256 Va. 19, 501 S. E. 2d 417, 418 (1998) (interpreting Virginia nonparental visitation statute to require finding of harm as condition precedent to awarding visitation).

Justice Stevens criticizes our reliance on what he characterizes as merely "a guess" about the Washington courts' interpretation of §26.10.160(3). Post, at 2. Justice Kennedy likewise states that "[m]ore specific guidance should await a case in which a State's highest court has considered all of the facts in the course of elaborating the protection afforded to parents by the laws of the State and by the Constitution itself." Post, at 10. We respectfully disagree. There is no need to hypothesize about how the Washington courts might apply §26.10.160(3) because the Washington Superior Court did apply the statute in this very case. Like the Washington Supreme Court, then, we are presented with an actual visitation order and the reasons why the Superior Court believed entry of the order was appropriate in this case. Faced with the Superior Court's application of §26.10.160(3) to Granville and her family, the Washington Supreme Court chose not to give the statute a narrower construction. Rather, that court gave §26.10.160(3) a literal and expansive interpretation. As we have explained, that broad construction plainly encompassed the Superior Court's application of the statute. See supra, at 8-9.

There is thus no reason to remand the case for further proceedings in the Washington Supreme Court. As Justice Kennedy recognizes, the burden of litigating a domestic relations proceeding can itself be "so disruptive of the parent-child relationship that the constitutional right of a custodial parent to make certain basic determinations for the child's welfare becomes implicated." Post at 9. In this case, the litigation costs incurred by Granville on her trip through the Washington court system and to this Court are without a doubt already substantial. As we have explained, it is apparent that the entry of the visitation order in this case violated the Constitution. We should say so now, without forcing the parties into additional litigation that would further burden Granville's parental right. We therefore hold that the application of §26.10.160(3) to Granville and her family violated her due process right to make decisions concerning the care, custody, and control of her daughters.

Accordingly, the judgment of the Washington Supreme Court is affirmed.

It is so ordered.

JENIFER TROXEL, et vir, PETITIONERS v. TOMMIE GRANVILLE
on writ of certiorari to the supreme court of Washington
[June 5, 2000]

Justice Souter, concurring in the judgment.

I concur in the judgment affirming the decision of the Supreme Court of Washington, whose facial invalidation of its own state statute is consistent with this Court's prior cases addressing the substantive interests at stake. I would say no more. The issues that might well be presented by reviewing a decision addressing the specific application of the state statute by the trial court, ante, at 9-14, are not before us and do not call for turning any fresh furrows in the "treacherous field" of substantive due process. Moore v. East Cleveland, 431 U. S. 494, 502 (1977) (opinion of Powell, J.).

The Supreme Court of Washington invalidated its state statute based on the text of the statute alone, not its application to any particular case.1 Its ruling rested on two independently sufficient grounds: the failure of the statute to require harm to the child to justify a disputed visitation order, In re Smith, 137 Wash. 2d, 1, 17, 969 P. 2d 21, 29 (1998), and the statute's authorization of "any person" at "any time" to petition and to receive visitation rights subject only to a free-ranging best-interests-of-the-child standard, id., at 20-21, 969 P. 2d, at 30-31. Ante, at 4. I see no error in the second reason, that because the state statute authorizes any person at any time to request (and a judge to award) visitation rights, subject only to the State's particular best-interests standard, the state statute sweeps too broadly and is unconstitutional on its face. Consequently, there is no need to decide whether harm is required or to consider the precise scope of the parent's right or its necessary protections.

We have long recognized that a parent's interests in the nurture, upbringing, companionship, care, and custody of children are generally protected by the Due Process Clause of the Fourteenth Amendment. See, e.g., Meyer v. Nebraska, 262 U. S. 390, 399, 401 (1923); Pierce v. Society of Sisters, 268 U. S. 510, 535 (1925); Stanley v. Illinois, 405 U. S. 645, 651 (1972); Wisconsin v. Yoder, 406 U. S. 205, 232 (1972); Quilloin v. Walcott, 434 U. S. 246, 255 (1978); Parham v. J. R., 442 U. S. 584, 602 (1979); Santosky v. Kramer, 455 U. S. 745, 753 (1982); Washington v. Glucksberg, 521 U. S. 702, 720 (1997). As we first acknowledged in Meyer, the right of parents to "bring up children," 262 U. S., at 399, and "to control the education of their own" is protected by the Constitution, id., at 401. See also Glucksberg, supra, at 761 (Souter, J., concurring in judgment).

On the basis of this settled principle, the Supreme Court of Washington invalidated its statute because it authorized a contested visitation order at the intrusive behest of any person at any time subject only to a best-interests-of-the-child standard. In construing the statute, the state court explained that the "any person" at "any time" language was to be read literally, at 137 Wash. 2d, at 10-11, 969 P. 2d, at 25-27, and that "[m]ost notably the statut[e] do[es] not require the petitioner to establish that he or she has a substantial relationship with the child," id., at 20-21, 969 P. 2d, at 31. Although the statute speaks of granting visitation rights whenever "visitation may serve the best interest of the child," Wash. Rev. Code §26.10.160(3) (1994), the state court authoritatively read this provision as placing hardly any limit on a court's discretion to award visitation rights. As the court understood it, the specific best-interests provision in the statute would allow a court to award visitation whenever it thought it could make a better decision than a child's parent had done. See 137 Wash. 2d, at 20, 969 P. 2d, at 31 ("It is not within the province of the state to make significant decisions concerning the custody of children merely because it could make a `better' decision").2 On that basis in part, the Supreme Court of Washington invalidated the State's own statute: "Parents have a right to limit visitation of their children with third persons." Id., at 21, 969 P. 2d, at 31.

Our cases, it is true, have not set out exact metes and bounds to the protected interest of a parent in the relationship with his child, but Meyer's repeatedly recognized right of upbringing would be a sham if it failed to encompass the right to be free of judicially compelled visitation by "any party" at "any time" a judge believed he "could make a `better' decision"3 than the objecting parent had done. The strength of a parent's interest in controlling a child's associates is as obvious as the influence of personal associations on the development of the child's social and moral character. Whether for good or for ill, adults not only influence but may indoctrinate children, and a choice about a child's social companions is not essentially different from the designation of the adults who will influence the child in school. Even a State's considered judgment about the preferable political and religious character of school-teachers is not entitled to prevail over a parent's choice of private school. Pierce, supra, at 535 ("The fundamental theory of liberty upon which all governments in this Union repose excludes any general power of the State to standardize its children by forcing them to accept instruction from public teachers only. The child is not the mere creature of the State; those who nurture him and direct his destiny have the right, coupled with the high duty, to recognize and prepare him for additional obligations"). It would be anomalous, then, to subject a parent to any individual judge's choice of a child's associates from out of the general population merely because the judge might think himself more enlightened than the child's parent.4 To say the least (and as the Court implied in Pierce), parental choice in such matters is not merely a default rule in the absence of either governmental choice or the government's designation of an official with the power to choose for whatever reason and in whatever circumstances.

Since I do not question the power of a State's highest court to construe its domestic statute and to apply a demanding standard when ruling on its facial constitutionality,5 see Chicago v. Morales, 527 U. S. 41, 55, n. 22 (1999) (opinion of Stevens, J.), this for me is the end of the case. I would simply affirm the decision of the Supreme Court of Washington that its statute, authorizing courts to grant visitation rights to any person at any time, is unconstitutional. I therefore respectfully concur in the judgment.

JENIFER TROXEL, et vir, PETITIONERS v.
TOMMIE GRANVILLE
on writ of certiorari to the supreme court
of Washington
[June 5, 2000]

Justice Thomas, concurring in the judgment.

I write separately to note that neither party has argued that our substantive due process cases were wrongly decided and that the original understanding of the Due Process Clause precludes judicial enforcement of unenumerated rights under that constitutional provision. As a result, I express no view on the merits of this matter, and I understand the plurality as well to leave the resolution of that issue for another day.*1

Consequently, I agree with the plurality that this Court's recognition of a fundamental right of parents to direct the upbringing of their children resolves this case. Our decision in Pierce v. Society of Sisters, 268 U. S. 510 (1925), holds that parents have a fundamental constitutional right to rear their children, including the right to determine who shall educate and socialize them. The opinions of the plurality, Justice Kennedy, and Justice Souter recognize such a right, but curiously none of them articulates the appropriate standard of review. I would apply strict scrutiny to infringements of fundamental rights. Here, the State of Washington lacks even a legitimate governmental interest—to say nothing of a compelling one—in second-guessing a fit parent's decision regarding visitation with third parties. On this basis, I would affirm the judgment below.

JENIFER TROXEL, et vir, PETITIONERS v.
TOMMIE GRANVILLE
on writ of certiorari to the supreme court
of Washington
[June 5, 2000]

Justice Stevens, dissenting.

The Court today wisely declines to endorse either the holding or the reasoning of the Supreme Court of Washington. In my opinion, the Court would have been even wiser to deny certiorari. Given the problematic character of the trial court's decision and the uniqueness of the Washington statute, there was no pressing need to review a State Supreme Court decision that merely requires the state legislature to draft a better statute.

Having decided to address the merits, however, the Court should begin by recognizing that the State Supreme Court rendered a federal constitutional judgment holding a state law invalid on its face. In light of that judgment, I believe that we should confront the federal questions presented directly. For the Washington statute is not made facially invalid either because it may be invoked by too many hypothetical plaintiffs, or because it leaves open the possibility that someone may be permitted to sustain a relationship with a child without having to prove that serious harm to the child would otherwise result.

I

In response to Tommie Granville's federal constitutional challenge, the State Supreme Court broadly held that Wash. Rev. Code §26.10.160(3) (Supp. 1996) was invalid on its face under the Federal Constitution.1 Despite the nature of this judgment, Justice O'Connor would hold that the Washington visitation statute violated the Due Process Clause of the Fourteenth Amendment only as applied. Ante, at 6, 8, 14-15. I agree with Justice Souter, ante, at 1, and n. 1 (opinion concurring in judgment), that this approach is untenable.

The task of reviewing a trial court's application of a state statute to the particular facts of a case is one that should be performed in the first instance by the state appellate courts. In this case, because of their views of the Federal Constitution, the Washington state appeals courts have yet to decide whether the trial court's findings were adequate under the statute.2 Any as-applied critique of the trial court's judgment that this Court might offer could only be based upon a guess about the state courts' application of that State's statute, and an independent assessment of the facts in this case—both judgments that we are ill-suited and ill-advised to make.3

While I thus agree with Justice Souter in this respect, I do not agree with his conclusion that the State Supreme Court made a definitive construction of the visitation statute that necessitates the constitutional conclusion he would draw.4 As I read the State Supreme Court's opinion, In re Smith, 137 Wash. 2d 1, 19-20, 969 P. 2d 21, 30-31 (1998), its interpretation of the Federal Constitution made it unnecessary to adopt a definitive construction of the statutory text, or, critically, to decide whether the statute had been correctly applied in this case. In particular, the state court gave no content to the phrase, "best interest of the child," Wash. Rev. Code §26.10.160(3) (Supp. 1996)—content that might well be gleaned from that State's own statutes or decisional law employing the same phrase in different contexts, and from the myriad other state statutes and court decisions at least nominally applying the same standard.5 Thus, I believe that Justice Souter's conclusion that the statute unconstitutionally imbues state trial court judges with "'too much discretion in every case,'" ante, at 4, n. 3 (opinion concurring in judgment) (quoting Chicago v. Morales, 527 U. S. 41, 71 (1999) (Breyer, J., concurring)), is premature.

We are thus presented with the unconstrued terms of a state statute and a State Supreme Court opinion that, in my view, significantly misstates the effect of the Federal Constitution upon any construction of that statute. Given that posture, I believe the Court should identify and correct the two flaws in the reasoning of the state court's majority opinion, and remand for further review of the trial court's disposition of this specific case.

II

In my view, the State Supreme Court erred in its federal constitutional analysis because neither the provision granting "any person" the right to petition the court for visitation, 137 Wash. 2d, at 20, 969 P. 2d, at 30, nor the absence of a provision requiring a "threshold ... finding of harm to the child," ibid., provides a sufficient basis for holding that the statute is invalid in all its applications. I believe that a facial challenge should fail whenever a statute has "a 'plainly legitimate sweep,'" Washington v. Glucksberg, 521 U. S. 702, 739-740 and n. 7 (1997) (Stevens, J., concurring in judgment).6 Under the Washington statute, there are plainly any number of cases—indeed, one suspects, the most common to arise—in which the "person" among "any" seeking visitation is a once-custodial caregiver, an intimate relation, or even a genetic parent. Even the Court would seem to agree that in many circumstances, it would be constitutionally permissible for a court to award some visitation of a child to a parent or previous caregiver in cases of parental separation or divorce, cases of disputed custody, cases involving temporary foster care or guardianship, and so forth. As the statute plainly sweeps in a great deal of the permissible, the State Supreme Court majority incorrectly concluded that a statute authorizing "any person" to file a petition seeking visitation privileges would invariably run afoul of the Fourteenth Amendment.

The second key aspect of the Washington Supreme Court's holding—that the Federal Constitution requires a showing of actual or potential "harm" to the child before a court may order visitation continued over a parent's objections—finds no support in this Court's case law. While, as the Court recognizes, the Federal Constitution certainly protects the parent-child relationship from arbitrary impairment by the State, see infra, at 7-8 we have never held that the parent's liberty interest in this relationship is so inflexible as to establish a rigid constitutional shield, protecting every arbitrary parental decision from any challenge absent a threshold finding of harm.7 The presumption that parental decisions generally serve the best interests of their children is sound, and clearly in the normal case the parent's interest is paramount. But even a fit parent is capable of treating a child like a mere possession.

Cases like this do not present a bipolar struggle between the parents and the State over who has final authority to determine what is in a child's best interests. There is at a minimum a third individual, whose interests are implicated in every case to which the statute applies—the child.

It has become standard practice in our substantive due process jurisprudence to begin our analysis with an identification of the "fundamental" liberty interests implicated by the challenged state action. See, e.g., ante, at 6-8 (opinion of O'Connor, J.); Washington v. Glucksberg, 521 U. S. 702 (1997); Planned Parenthood of Southeastern Pa. v. Casey, 505 U. S. 833 (1992). My colleagues are of course correct to recognize that the right of a parent to maintain a relationship with his or her child is among the interests included most often in the constellation of liberties protected through the Fourteenth Amendment. Ante, at 6-8 (opinion of O'Connor, J.). Our cases leave no doubt that parents have a fundamental liberty interest in caring for and guiding their children, and a corresponding privacy interest—absent exceptional circumstances—in doing so without the undue interference of strangers to them and to their child. Moreover, and critical in this case, our cases applying this principle have explained that with this constitutional liberty comes a presumption (albeit a rebuttable one) that "natural bonds of affection lead parents to act in the best interests of their children." Parham v. J. R., 442 U. S. 584, 602 (1979); see also Casey, 505 U.S., at 895; Santosky v. Kramer, 455 U. S. 745, 759 (1982) (State may not presume, at fact-finding stage of parental rights termination proceeding, that interests of parent and child diverge); see also ante, at 9-10 (opinion of O'Connor, J.).

Despite this Court's repeated recognition of these significant parental liberty interests, these interests have never been seen to be without limits. In Lehr v. Robertson, 463 U. S. 248 (1983), for example, this Court held that a putative biological father who had never established an actual relationship with his child did not have a constitutional right to notice of his child's adoption by the man who had married the child's mother. As this Court had recognized in an earlier case, a parent's liberty interests "'do not spring full-blown from the biological connection between parent and child. They require relationships more enduring.'" Id., at 260 (quoting Caban v. Mohammed, 441 U. S. 380, 397 (1979)).

Conversely, in Michael H. v. Gerald D., 491 U. S. 110 (1989), this Court concluded that despite both biological parenthood and an established relationship with a young child, a father's due process liberty interest in maintaining some connection with that child was not sufficiently powerful to overcome a state statutory presumption that the husband of the child's mother was the child's parent. As a result of the presumption, the biological father could be denied even visitation with the child because, as a matter of state law, he was not a "parent." A plurality of this Court there recognized that the parental liberty interest was a function, not simply of "isolated factors" such as biology and intimate connection, but of the broader and apparently independent interest in family. See, e.g. . id., at 123; see also Lehr, 463 U. S., at 261; Smith v. Organization of Foster Families For Equality & Reform, 431 U. S. 816, 842-847 (1977); Moore v. East Cleveland, 431 U. S. 494, 498-504 (1977).

A parent's rights with respect to her child have thus never been regarded as absolute, but rather are limited by the existence of an actual, developed relationship with a child, and are tied to the presence or absence of some embodiment of family. These limitations have arisen, not simply out of the definition of parenthood itself, but because of this Court's assumption that a parent's interests in a child must be balanced against the State's long-recognized interests as parens patriae, see, e.g., Reno v. Flores, 507 U. S. 292, 303-304 (1993); Santosky v. Kramer, 455 U. S., at 766; Parham, 442 U.S., at 605; Prince v. Massachusetts, 321 U. S. 158, 166 (1944), and, critically, the child's own complementary interest in preserving relationships that serve her welfare and protection, Santosky, 455 U. S., at 760.

While this Court has not yet had occasion to elucidate the nature of a child's liberty interests in preserving established familial or family-like bonds, 491 U. S., at 130 (reserving the question), it seems to me extremely likely that, to the extent parents and families have fundamental liberty interests in preserving such intimate relationships, so, too, do children have these interests, and so, too, must their interests be balanced in the equation.8 At a minimum, our prior cases recognizing that children are, generally speaking, constitutionally protected actors require that this Court reject any suggestion that when it comes to parental rights, children are so much chattel. See ante, at 5-6 (opinion of O'Connor, J.) (describing States' recognition of "an independent third-party interest in a child"). The constitutional protection against arbitrary state interference with parental rights should not be extended to prevent the States from protecting children against the arbitrary exercise of parental authority that is not in fact motivated by an interest in the welfare of the child.9

This is not, of course, to suggest that a child's liberty interest in maintaining contact with a particular individual is to be treated invariably as on a par with that child's parents' contrary interests. Because our substantive due process case law includes a strong presumption that a parent will act in the best interest of her child, it would be necessary, were the state appellate courts actually to confront a challenge to the statute as applied, to consider whether the trial court's assessment of the "best interest of the child" incorporated that presumption. Neither would I decide whether the trial court applied Washington's statute in a constitutional way in this case, although, as I have explained, n. 3, supra, I think the outcome of this determination is far from clear. For the purpose of a facial challenge like this, I think it safe to assume that trial judges usually give great deference to parents' wishes, and I am not persuaded otherwise here.

But presumptions notwithstanding, we should recognize that there may be circumstances in which a child has a stronger interest at stake than mere protection from serious harm caused by the termination of visitation by a "person" other than a parent. The almost infinite variety of family relationships that pervade our ever-changing society strongly counsel against the creation by this Court of a constitutional rule that treats a biological parent's liberty interest in the care and supervision of her child as an isolated right that may be exercised arbitrarily. It is indisputably the business of the States, rather than a federal court employing a national standard, to assess in the first instance the relative importance of the conflicting interests that give rise to disputes such as this.10 Far from guaranteeing that parents' interests will be trammeled in the sweep of cases arising under the statute, the Washington law merely gives an individual—with whom a child may have an established relationship—the procedural right to ask the

State to act as arbiter, through the entirely well-known best-interests standard, between the parent's protected interests and the child's. It seems clear to me that the Due Process Clause of the Fourteenth Amendment leaves room for States to consider the impact on a child of possibly arbitrary parental decisions that neither serve nor are motivated by the best interests of the child.

Accordingly, I respectfully dissent.

JENIFER TROXEL, et vir, PETITIONERS v.
TOMMIE GRANVILLE
on writ of certiorari to the supreme court
of Washington
[June 5, 2000]

Justice Scalia, dissenting.

In my view, a right of parents to direct the upbringing of their children is among the "unalienable Rights" with which the Declaration of Independence proclaims "all Men ... are endowed by their Creator." And in my view that right is also among the "othe[r] [rights] retained by the people" which the Ninth Amendment says the Constitution's enumeration of rights "shall not be construed to deny or disparage." The Declaration of Independence, however, is not a legal prescription conferring powers upon the courts; and the Constitution's refusal to "deny or disparage" other rights is far removed from affirming any one of them, and even farther removed from authorizing judges to identify what they might be, and to enforce the judges' list against laws duly enacted by the people. Consequently, while I would think it entirely compatible with the commitment to representative democracy set forth in the founding documents to argue, in legislative chambers or in electoral campaigns, that the state has no power to interfere with parents' authority over the rearing of their children, I do not believe that the power which the Constitution confers upon me as a judge entitles me to deny legal effect to laws that (in my view) infringe upon what is (in my view) that unenumerated right.

Only three holdings of this Court rest in whole or in part upon a substantive constitutional right of parents to direct the upbringing of their children1—two of them from an era rich in substantive due process holdings that have since been repudiated. See Meyer v. Nebraska, 262 U. S. 390, 399, 401 (1923); Pierce v. Society of Sisters, 268 U. S. 510, 534-535 (1925); Wisconsin v. Yoder, 406 U. S. 205, 232-233 (1972). Cf. West Coast Hotel Co. v. Parrish, 300 U. S. 379 (1937) (overruling Adkins v. Children's Hospital of D. C., 261 U. S. 525 (1923)). The sheer diversity of today's opinions persuades me that the theory of unenumerated parental rights underlying these three cases has small claim to stare decisis protection. A legal principle that can be thought to produce such diverse outcomes in the relatively simple case before us here is not a legal principle that has induced substantial reliance. While I would not now overrule those earlier cases (that has not been urged), neither would I extend the theory upon which they rested to this new context.

Judicial vindication of "parental rights" under a Constitution that does not even mention them requires (as Justice Kennedy's opinion rightly points out) not only a judicially crafted definition of parents, but also—unless, as no one believes, the parental rights are to be absolute—judicially approved assessments of "harm to the child" and judicially defined gradations of other persons (grandparents, extended family, adoptive family in an adoption later found to be invalid, long-term guardians, etc.) who may have some claim against the wishes of the parents. If we embrace this unenumerated right, I think it obvious—whether we affirm or reverse the judgment here, or remand as Justice Stevens or Justice Kennedy would do—that we will be ushering in a new regime of judicially prescribed, and federally prescribed, family law. I have no reason to believe that federal judges will be better at this than state legislatures; and state legislatures have the great advantages of doing harm in a more circumscribed area, of being able to correct their mistakes in a flash, and of being removable by the people.2

For these reasons, I would reverse the judgment below.

JENIFER TROXEL, et vir, PETITIONERS v.
TOMMIE GRANVILLE
on writ of certiorari to the supreme court
of Washington
[June 5, 2000]

Justice Kennedy, dissenting.

The Supreme Court of Washington has determined that petitioners Jenifer and Gary Troxel have standing under state law to seek court-ordered visitation with their grandchildren, notwithstanding the objections of the children's parent, respondent Tommie Granville. The statute relied upon provides:

"Any person may petition the court for visitation rights at any time including, but not limited to, custody proceedings. The court may order visitation rights for any person when visitation may serve the best interest of the child whether or not there has been any change of circumstances." Wash. Rev. Code §26.10.160(3) (1994).

After acknowledging this statutory right to sue for visitation, the State Supreme Court invalidated the statute as violative of the United States Constitution, because it interfered with a parent's right to raise his or her child free from unwarranted interference. In re Smith, 137 Wash. 2d 1, 969 P. 2d 21 (1998). Although parts of the court's decision may be open to differing interpretations, it seems to be agreed that the court invalidated the statute on its face, ruling it a nullity.

The first flaw the State Supreme Court found in the statute is that it allows an award of visitation to a non-parent without a finding that harm to the child would result if visitation were withheld; and the second is that the statute allows any person to seek visitation at any time. In my view the first theory is too broad to be correct, as it appears to contemplate that the best interests of the child standard may not be applied in any visitation case. I acknowledge the distinct possibility that visitation cases may arise where, considering the absence of other protection for the parent under state laws and procedures, the best interests of the child standard would give insufficient protection to the parent's constitutional right to raise the child without undue intervention by the state; but it is quite a different matter to say, as I understand the Supreme Court of Washington to have said, that a harm to the child standard is required in every instance.

Given the error I see in the State Supreme Court's central conclusion that the best interests of the child standard is never appropriate in third-party visitation cases, that court should have the first opportunity to reconsider this case. I would remand the case to the state court for further proceedings. If it then found the statute has been applied in an unconstitutional manner because the best interests of the child standard gives insufficient protection to a parent under the circumstances of this case, or if it again declared the statute a nullity because the statute seems to allow any person at all to seek visitation at any time, the decision would present other issues which may or may not warrant further review in this Court. These include not only the protection the Constitution gives parents against state-ordered visitation but also the extent to which federal rules for facial challenges to statutes control in state courts. These matters, however, should await some further case. The judgment now under review should be vacated and remanded on the sole ground that the harm ruling that was so central to the Supreme Court of Washington's decision was error, given its broad formulation.

Turning to the question whether harm to the child must be the controlling standard in every visitation proceeding, there is a beginning point that commands general, perhaps unanimous, agreement in our separate opinions: As our case law has developed, the custodial parent has a constitutional right to determine, without undue interference by the state, how best to raise, nurture, and educate the child. The parental right stems from the liberty protected by the Due Process Clause of the Fourteenth Amendment. See, e.g., Meyer v. Nebraska, 262 U. S. 390, 399, 401 (1923); Pierce v. Society of Sisters, 268 U. S. 510, 534-535 (1925); Prince v. Massachusetts, 321 U. S. 158, 166 (1944); Stanley v. Illinois, 405 U. S. 645, 651-652 (1972); Wisconsin v. Yoder, 406 U. S. 205, 232-233 (1972); Santosky v. Kramer, 455 U. S. 745, 753-754 (1982). Pierce and Meyer, had they been decided in recent times, may well have been grounded upon First Amendment principles protecting freedom of speech, belief, and religion. Their formulation and subsequent interpretation have been quite different, of course; and they long have been interpreted to have found in Fourteenth Amendment concepts of liberty an independent right of the parent in the "custody, care and nurture of the child," free from state intervention. Prince, supra, at 166. The principle exists, then, in broad formulation; yet courts must use considerable restraint, including careful adherence to the incremental instruction given by the precise facts of particular cases, as they seek to give further and more precise definition to the right.

The State Supreme Court sought to give content to the parent's right by announcing a categorical rule that third parties who seek visitation must always prove the denial of visitation would harm the child. After reviewing some of the relevant precedents, the Supreme Court of Washington concluded " `[t]he requirement of harm is the sole protection that parents have against pervasive state interference in the parenting process.' " In re Smith, 137 Wash. 2d, at 19-20, 969 P. 2d, at 30 (quoting Hawk v. Hawk, 855 S. W. 2d 573, 580 (Tenn. 1993)). For that reason, "[s]hort of preventing harm to the child," the court considered the best interests of the child to be "insufficient to serve as a compelling state interest overruling a parent's fundamental rights." In re Smith, supra, at 20, 969 P. 2d, at 30.

While it might be argued as an abstract matter that in some sense the child is always harmed if his or her best interests are not considered, the law of domestic relations, as it has evolved to this point, treats as distinct the two standards, one harm to the child and the other the best interests of the child. The judgment of the Supreme Court of Washington rests on that assumption, and I, too, shall assume that there are real and consequential differences between the two standards.

On the question whether one standard must always take precedence over the other in order to protect the right of the parent or parents, "[o]ur Nation's history, legal traditions, and practices" do not give us clear or definitive answers. Washington v. Glucksberg, 521 U. S. 702, 721 (1997). The consensus among courts and commentators is that at least through the 19th century there was no legal right of visitation; court-ordered visitation appears to be a 20th-century phenomenon. See, e.g., 1 D. Kramer, Legal Rights of Children 124, 136 (2d ed. 1994); 2 J. Atkinson, Modern Child Custody Practice §8.10 (1986). A case often cited as one of the earliest visitation decisions, Succession of Reiss, 46 La. Ann. 347, 353, 15 So. 151, 152 (1894), explained that "the obligation ordinarily to visit grandparents is moral and not legal"—a conclusion which appears consistent with that of American common law jurisdictions of the time. Early 20th-century exceptions did occur, often in cases where a relative had acted in a parental capacity, or where one of a child's parents had died. See Douglass v. Merriman, 163 S. C. 210, 161 S. E. 452 (1931) (maternal grandparent awarded visitation with child when custody was awarded to father; mother had died); Solomon v. Solomon, 319 Ill. App. 618, 49 N. E. 2d 807 (1943) (paternal grandparents could be given visitation with child in custody of his mother when their son was stationed abroad; case remanded for fitness hearing); Consaul v. Consaul, 63 N. Y. S. 2d 688 (Sup. Ct. Jefferson Cty. 1946) (paternal grandparents awarded visitation with child in custody of his mother; father had become incompetent). As a general matter, however, contemporary state-court decisions acknowledge that "[h]istorically, grandparents had no legal right of visitation," Campbell v. Campbell, 896 P. 2d 635, 642, n. 15 (Utah App. 1995), and it is safe to assume other third parties would have fared no better in court.

To say that third parties have had no historical right to petition for visitation does not necessarily imply, as the Supreme Court of Washington concluded, that a parent has a constitutional right to prevent visitation in all cases not involving harm. True, this Court has acknowledged that States have the authority to intervene to prevent harm to children, see, e.g., Prince, supra, at 168-169; Yoder, supra, at 233-234, but that is not the same as saying that a heightened harm to the child standard must be satisfied in every case in which a third party seeks a visitation order. It is also true that the law's traditional presumption has been "that natural bonds of affection lead parents to act in the best interests of their children," Parham v. J. R., 442 U. S. 584, 602 (1979); and "[s]imply because the decision of a parent is not agreeable to a child or because it involves risks does not automatically transfer the power to make that decision from the parents to some agency or officer of the state," id., at 603. The State Supreme Court's conclusion that the Constitution forbids the application of the best interests of the child standard in any visitation proceeding, however, appears to rest upon assumptions the Constitution does not require.

My principal concern is that the holding seems to proceed from the assumption that the parent or parents who resist visitation have always been the child's primary caregivers and that the third parties who seek visitation have no legitimate and established relationship with the child. That idea, in turn, appears influenced by the concept that the conventional nuclear family ought to establish the visitation standard for every domestic relations case. As we all know, this is simply not the structure or prevailing condition in many households. See, e.g., Moore v. East Cleveland, 431 U. S. 494 (1977). For many boys and girls a traditional family with two or even one permanent and caring parent is simply not the reality of their childhood. This may be so whether their childhood has been marked by tragedy or filled with considerable happiness and fulfillment.

Cases are sure to arise—perhaps a substantial number of cases—in which a third party, by acting in a caregiving role over a significant period of time, has developed a relationship with a child which is not necessarily subject to absolute parental veto. See Michael H. v. Gerald D., 491 U. S. 110

(1989) (putative natural father not entitled to rebut state law presumption that child born in a marriage is a child of the marriage); Quilloin v. Walcott, 434 U. S. 246 (1978) (best interests standard sufficient in adoption proceeding to protect interests of natural father who had not legitimated the child); see also Lehr v. Robertson, 463 U. S. 248, 261 (1983) (" `[T]he importance of the familial relationship, to the individuals involved and to the society, stems from the emotional attachments that derive from the intimacy of daily association, and from the role it plays in 'promot[ing] a way of life' through the instruction of children ... as well as from the fact of blood relationship.'" (quoting Smith v. Organization of Foster Families For Equality & Reform, 431 U. S. 816, 844 (1977) (in turn quoting Yoder, 406 U. S., at 231-233))). Some pre-existing relationships, then, serve to identify persons who have a strong attachment to the child with the concomitant motivation to act in a responsible way to ensure the child's welfare. As the State Supreme Court was correct to acknowledge, those relationships can be so enduring that "in certain circumstances where a child has enjoyed a substantial relationship with a third person, arbitrarily depriving the child of the relationship could cause severe psychological harm to the child," In re Smith, 137 Wash. 2d, at 20, 969 P. 2d, at 30; and harm to the adult may also ensue. In the design and elaboration of their visitation laws, States may be entitled to consider that certain relationships are such that to avoid the risk of harm, a best interests standard can be employed by their domestic relations courts in some circumstances.

Indeed, contemporary practice should give us some pause before rejecting the best interests of the child standard in all third-party visitation cases, as the Washington court has done. The standard has been recognized for many years as a basic tool of domestic relations law in visitation proceedings.

Since 1965 all 50 States have enacted a third-party visitation statute of some sort. See ante, at 15, n. (plurality opinion). Each of these statutes, save one, permits a court order to issue in certain cases if visitation is found to be in the best interests of the child. While it is unnecessary for us to consider the constitutionality of any particular provision in the case now before us, it can be noted that the statutes also include a variety of methods for limiting parents' exposure to third-party visitation petitions and for ensuring parental decisions are given respect. Many States limit the identity of permissible petitioners by restricting visitation petitions to grandparents, or by requiring petitioners to show a substantial relationship with a child, or both. See, e.g., Kan. Stat. Ann. §38-129 (1993 and Supp. 1998) (grandparent visitation authorized under certain circumstances if a substantial relationship exists); N. C. Gen. Stat. §§50-13.2, 50-13.2A, 50-13.5 (1999) (same); Iowa Code §598.35 (Supp. 1999) (same; visitation also authorized for great-grandparents); Wis. Stat. §767.245 (Supp. 1999) (visitation authorized under certain circumstances for "a grandparent, greatgrandparent, stepparent or person who has maintained a relationship similar to a parent-child relationship with the child"). The statutes vary in other respects—for instance, some permit visitation petitions when there has been a change in circumstances such as divorce or death of a parent, see, e.g., N. H. Rev. Stat. Ann. §458:17-d (1992), and some apply a presumption that parental decisions should control, see, e.g., Cal. Fam. Code Ann. §§3104(e)-(f) (West 1994); R. I. Gen. Laws §15-5-24.3(a)(2)(v) (Supp. 1999). Georgia's is the sole State Legislature to have adopted a general harm to the child standard, see Ga. Code Ann. §19-7-3(c) (1999), and it did so only after the Georgia Supreme Court held the State's prior visitation statute invalid under the Federal and Georgia Constitutions, see Brooks v. Parkerson, 265 Ga. 189, 454 S. E. 2d 769, cert. denied, 516 U. S. 942 (1995).

In light of the inconclusive historical record and case law, as well as the almost universal adoption of the best interests standard for visitation disputes, I would be hard pressed to conclude the right to be free of such review in all cases is itself " `implicit in the concept of ordered liberty.' " Glucksberg, 521 U. S., at 721 (quoting Palko v. Connecticut, 302 U. S. 319, 325 (1937)). In my view, it would be more appropriate to conclude that the constitutionality of the application of the best interests standard depends on more specific factors. In short, a fit parent's right vis-à-vis a complete stranger is one thing; her right vis-à-vis another parent or a de facto parent may be another. The protection the Constitution requires, then, must be elaborated with care, using the discipline and instruction of the case law system. We must keep in mind that family courts in the 50 States confront these factual variations each day, and are best situated to consider the unpredictable, yet inevitable, issues that arise. Cf. Ankenbrandt v. Richards, 504 U. S. 689, 703-704 (1992).

It must be recognized, of course, that a domestic relations proceeding in and of itself can constitute state intervention that is so disruptive of the parent-child relationship that the constitutional right of a custodial parent to make certain basic determinations for the child's welfare becomes implicated. The best interests of the child standard has at times been criticized as indeterminate, leading to unpredictable results. See, e.g., American Law Institute, Principles of the Law of Family Dissolution 2, and n. 2 (Tentative Draft No. 3, Mar. 20, 1998). If a single parent who is struggling to raise a child is faced with visitation demands from a third party, the attorney's fees alone might destroy her hopes and plans for the child's future. Our system must confront more often the reality that litigation can itself be so disruptive that constitutional protection may be required; and I do not discount the possibility that in some instances the best interests of the child standard may provide insufficient protection to the parent-child relationship. We owe it to the Nation's domestic relations legal structure, however, to proceed with caution.

It should suffice in this case to reverse the holding of the State Supreme Court that the application of the best interests of the child standard is always unconstitutional in third-party visitation cases. Whether, under the circumstances of this case, the order requiring visitation over the objection of this fit parent violated the Constitution ought to be reserved for further proceedings. Because of its sweeping ruling requiring the harm to the child standard, the Supreme Court of Washington did not have the occasion to address the specific visitation order the Troxels obtained. More specific guidance should await a case in which a State's highest court has considered all of the facts in the course of elaborating the protection afforded to parents by the laws of the State and by the Constitution itself. Furthermore, in my view, we need not address whether, under the correct constitutional standards, the Washington statute can be invalidated on its face. This question, too, ought to be addressed by the state court in the first instance.

In my view the judgment under review should be vacated and the case remanded for further proceedings.

13

New Grandparents

"You will never stand so tall as when you sit reading with your grandchild." ~NEIL TAFT

Having named this book *No Greater Loss* causes me to consider naming this chapter "No Greater Joy." Ahhhhh! The birth of that first grandchild.

I can still clearly recall the exact moment that my daughter gave us the gift of Zak. While I marveled at the birth of my son and daughter, when Zak was born I remember that I savored that experience in a unique and special way. Instead of just counting those fingers and toes I was in awe of the miracle of those most delicate and intricate features of my new buddy. The sheer wonder of this little guy was made more perfect by time and maturity. This experience was much richer because I knew I had earned the title of Grandpa Neil.

This was a long-term deal between Zak (now 21) and me. We have books to read, fish to catch, trips to take, cars to fix, and stories to create together. My children were the cake that sustained me but my first grandchild added the icing on that cake. At the time I remember thinking that this is what life is all about, and years later it happened all over again when my daughter-in-law gave us the gift of Ceili (now 5).

I have written this book to give grandparents a heads-up on the things that can happen when families splinter and fracture. This chapter is about the things that we can create and foster that will make it less likely that we will have to assert our grandparents' rights. It will also help establish the ever so important bond between grandparent and grandchild.

This bond is essential on several levels. It is the greatest gift we can give our grandchild and ourselves. Too many grandparents feel they have moved into the phase of life when nothing seems as good as it once was. Your grandkids make sure you never grow out of touch, even while you enrich their lives.

This type of relationship with your grandchildren is also the first thing that the legal system requires if something goes wrong and you need to pursue your rights through legal channels. Admittedly it's something we don't want to think about but a necessity nevertheless.

As New Grandparents you are still very active in your own lives, and this new venture is ripe with opportunities for joy and fun. Enjoy these times and at the same time be aware of the societal changes that may affect you in the future.

Keep your memories close, and just know that they can also serve as records of the "significant impact" you have had in your grandchild's life in the unfortunate event you ever have to use them.

Photos and Videos: Memories and Records

The single most effective activity that brings a lot of joyful memories is filling the photo/video albums we love so much. This is one method of documenting your times with your grandchildren that at the same time illustrates the bonds between you and those beautiful little bundles of fun. I pray that you never have to use these wonderful memories to show some judge that you have had a long and mutually beneficial relationship with your grandchild, but if you do, this is one of the best ways to accomplish that task. There are other things to think about as time progresses and they can be found in the best practices chapters of this book.

Telephones and Cell Phones

Kids are on the phone today more than ever and at a younger age. The popularity of cell phones has reached far down into our youth, so that this upcoming generation thinks no more of picking up the phone and making a call than we would have turning on the TV. And kids today are more likely to answer the phone and use it for communication than any previous generation.

Making and receiving calls from your grandchildren is wonderful, especially if long distance separates you. It is no substitute for physical visitation but can fill the void between those times. If you share phone conversations with your grandchildren, make a simple text record of when the calls were and how long they lasted. This only takes a second, but such contact can help be a record of your importance in their lives should you ever need it.

Social Media: Emails and Facebook

Many of today's grandparents (see Grand-Boomers below) are still in the workforce so computers are more readily available and familiar to them. However, I get a lot of response from more mature folks (older grandparents) on all forms of social media. I think the veil has been lifted for our generation and computer use is becoming much more prevalent amongst our age group each and every year.

You now see many grandparents (especially Grand-Boomers) on social media such as Twitter and Facebook. Facebook is particularly liked and appropriate for people new to social media because unlike simple interactions on forums or blogs or message boards, you are allowed to easily choose who your "friends" are and who has access to your page and photos and postings. This makes it a more private way to communicate with your grandchildren and keep up with them through either their parents' pages or, if they are old enough, their own.

Barring direct email, Facebook is probably the safest and easiest of the social media to master. Just be aware that none of the online tools match personal interaction with your children and grandchildren, nor can you ever be assured of 100 percent privacy. Within that context, however, if you do have interactions such as emails or Facebook posts and messages with your grandchildren, always keep a copy as a record of them.

Websites and Current Information (for You)

Another reason for grandparents to be computer savvy and on the Internet is to take advantage of all the information and resources available to them. This very book grew out of a successful website (www.CaringGrandparents.com) which provides information, resources, hope, and advice to grandparents, many who are having difficulties seeing their grandchildren or dealing with visitation and custody issues. While print resources (like this one) are very important, there is no better way to keep up with the day-to-day happenings in grandparents' rights than such Internet sites, which also provide email addresses and ways for you to interact and ask your own questions.

Who Are the Grand-Boomers?

By definition the Baby Boomers were born between 1946 and 1964. That places them as grandparents right into the demographic according to the AARP 2002 Grandparents Study.

Since the average age for a new grandparent is now 48, we have just added a lot of folks to our group. We presently comprise one-third of the adult population in the United States. That is an enormous amount of wisdom held by a group of folks that love to share it with their grandkids.

The Grand-Boomers generation of grandparents is a little younger, a little more physically active with the grandchildren, a little more educated (50 percent have attended or graduated from college) and a little more affluent according to this study. However, this generation is also more vulnerable to grandparents' custody and grandparents' visitation issues based on the present 50 percent divorce rate.

No one thinks it will happen to them but it is prudent for each of us to become well versed in grandparents' rights in the state where the grandkids reside as well as the current overall state of grandparents' rights.

Enough of the worry; just be aware of the possibility and do what you can now just in case.

The Roles of New Grandparents

The roles that accompany new grandparents are important and can be one of the rewards of getting older, as well as for the kids one of the rewards of being young.

Think of some of the roles that grandparents play in their grandchildren's lives. Often they help develop the value systems and personal identities of their grandchildren. They can teach their grandchildren about family history and tradition through stories and conversations. They can provide a sounding board for their grandchildren.

Grand-Boomers tend to travel more and that means more frequent visits with the grandchildren. The present trend shows that all grandparents are increasing their use of computers, which allows them to interact with the grandchildren on a medium that is more natural to the kids (see the information on social media, above).

Simply being a good listener and providing a sympathetic ear can help a grandchild express his or her feelings in a healthy manner. Grandparents and grandchildren are more like friends; children often feel freer to confide in them. This especially holds true when a child and his or her parents are going through times of familial discord.

I happen to believe that as grandparents we can bring something to a child's development and education that considerably enhances what the parents teach their children. Yes, I realize that we may spoil them just a wee bit, but any Caring Grandparent knows to use their considerable influence to reinforce the knowledge and values that the parents are teaching. The word that comes to mind is TRUST.

As a Youth Minister I always told the parents that it was valuable for their kids to have a significant adult, other than their parents, in their lives. In many cases this becomes a grandparent. What an honor and a responsibility for each of us to carry out. Just keep in mind that "what you do speaks so loud they can't hear what you are saying." Leading by example is not just the right way; it is the only way.

I savor each of my 6 grandchildren. Each is so very different and my interaction with each is so very different, but my stewardship of a trusting relationship is foremost in my mind whenever I pick up the phone or spend time with any and/or all of them. It is indeed a higher calling to be a good and Caring Grandparent, and the rewards are instantaneous and at the same time timeless.

A Caring life is so abundant and fun. Be Happy and Healthy.

14

Caring Grandparents: Resources

Caring Grandparents
www.caringgrandparents.com

AARP
601 E Street NW
Washington, DC 20049
888-OUR-AARP
www.aarp.org

Grandparents Rights Organization
100 West Long Lake Road
Suite 250
Bloomfield Hills
248-646-7177
www.grandparentsrights.org

Grandparents Magazine
www.grandparentsmagazine.net

Grandparents for Children's Rights

www.uwex.edu/ces/gprg/qandas.html

Grandparents Resource Center
grc4usa.org

Grandparents Today
grandparentstoday.org

Grandparents Raising Grandchildren
www.raisingyourgrandchildren.com

GRAND magazine
www.grandmagazine.com

Grandparents United DE, Inc.
grandparentsunitedde.org

Grandparent's Web
www.cyberparent.com/gran

National Adoption Information Clearinghouse
330 C Street, SW
Washington, DC 20447
703-352-3488
naic.acf.hhs.gov

BOOKS

Canfield, Jack & Hansen, Mark Victor. *Chicken Soup for the Soul: Grand and Great.* Chicken Soup for the Soul Publishing, 2008.

Covey, Stephen. *The 7 Habits of Highly Effective Families.* New York: St. Martin's, 1998.

Kornhaber, Arthur. *The Grandparents Solution. Jossey-Boss.* 2004.

Faber, Adele & Mazlish, Elaine. *How To Talk So Kids Will Listen and Listen So Kids Will Talk.* London: Picadilly Press, 2001.

Truly/ Traci. *Grandparents' Rights.* Sphinx Publishing, 2005.

Ellis, Helene LaBrecque. *A KINSHIP Guide to Rescuing Children.* 2008.

Maisel, Roberta. *All Grown Up: Living Happily Ever After With Your Adult Children.* Gabriola Island, BC: New Society, 2001.

Doucette-Dudman, Deborah. *Raising Our Children's Children.* Fairview Press, 1997.

De Toledo, Sylvie. ***Grandparents as Parents: A Survival Guide for Raising a Second Family.*** Guilford Press, 1995.

Chase, Giraurd. ***Pilgrim Prayers for Grandmothers Raising Grandchildren.*** Hollies Pilgrim Press, 2002.

Carson. Dr. Lillian. ***The Essential Grandparent.*** Heath Communications, 1996.

Carson. Dr. Lillian. ***The Essential Grandparent's Guide to Divorce.*** Heath Communications, 1999.

Slorah, Dr. Patricia. ***Grandparent's Rights.*** 2003

General Information

www.grandkidsandme.com
www.grandloving.com
www.grandboomers.com
www.childrensdefense.org

American Bar Association

www.abanet.org
www.findlaw.com

General Information and Legal Aspects of Grandparents Raising Grandchildren

www.raisingyourgrandchildren.com
www.grandparents-r-us.com
caregiving.org
www.aoa.gov
www.grandsplace.com
www.brookdalefoundation.org
www.grandparenting.org
www.fullcirclecare.org
www.essentialgrandparent.com
www.grandparentchildconnec.org
www.grandparentsforchildren.org
www.grandparentsasparents.com
http://prisonerswithchildren.org

Child Development

http://www.childdevelopmentinfo.com/
www.zerotothree.org
www.nichd.nih.gov
www.aboutourkids.org

Addiction Services

www.aa.org
www.helpguide.org

ALANON /ALATEEN
www.al-anon.org 1-888-4AL-ANON (888-425-2666)

National Institute on Drug Abuse
www.nida.nih.gov

Substance Abuse and Mental Health Services Administration
www.ncadi.samhsa.gov

MADD (Mothers Against Drunk Driving)
www.madd.org

American Council for Drug Education
www.acde.org

Alcoholics Anonymous
www.aa.org

Drug Free Info
www.drugfreeinfo.org

ADDITIONAL BOOKS

The Complete Book of Personal Legal Forms by Mark Warda and James Ray (Paperback - June 1, 2005)

Grandparent Visitation Rights: A Legal Research Guide (Legal Research Guides, Vol. 40) by M. Kristine Taylor Warren (Hardcover - Dec. 2000)

Between Parents and Grandparents by Arthur Kornhaber (Paperback - Feb 1989)

Grandparents/Grandch... by Arthur Kornhaber and Kenneth L. Woodward (Paperback - Jan. 1, 1984)
Spirit, St Martin's Press 1988

Grandparents, Grandchildren: The Vital Connection by Arthur Kornhaber (Hardcover - Mar 1981)

Grandparent Power!: How to Strengthen the Vital Connection Among Grandparents, Parents, and Children by Arthur Kornhaber M.D. and Sondra Forsyth (Paperback - Sept. 26, 1995)

Contemporary Grandparenting by Arthur Kornhaber (Paperback - Dec 7, 1995)

The Grandparent Guide : The Definitive Guide to Coping with the Challenges of Modern Grandparenting by Arthur Kornhaber (Paperback - Jun 20, 2002)

A Grandparent's Little Instruction Book (Little instruction books) by Jasmine Birtles (Paperback - Nov. 1, 1997)

When Your Grandparent Dies: A Child's Guide to Good Grief (Elf-Help Books for Kids) by Victoria Ryan and R. W. Alley (Paperback - Jun 2002)

Buzzed: The Straight Facts About the Most Used and Abused Drugs from Alcohol to Ecstasy (Third Edition) by Cynthia Kuhn, Scott Swartzwelder, and Wilkie Wilson (Paperback - Aug 17, 2008)

Clinical Supervision in Alcohol and Drug Abuse Counseling: Principles, Models, Methods by David J. Powell and Archie Brodsky (Paperback - May 20, 2004)

Illegal Drugs: A Complete Guide to their History, Chemistry, Use, and Abuse by Paul M. Gahlinger (Paperback - Dec 30, 2003)

When Someone You Love Abuses Drugs or Alcohol: Daily Encouragement by Cecil B. Murphey (Paperback - Sep 1, 2004)

How to Quit Drugs for Good: A Complete Self-Help Guide by Jerry Dorsman (Paperback - Oct 28, 1998)

Karch's Pathology of Drug Abuse, Fourth Edition by Steven B. Karch (Hardcover - Dec 15, 2008)

The Addiction Workbook: A Step-By-Step Guide to Quitting Alcohol and Drugs (New Harbinger Workbooks) by Patrick Fanning and John Terence O'Neill (Paperback - Jun 1996)

Understanding Your Special Needs Grandchild: A Grand-parent's Guide by Clare B. Jones (Paperback - Apr 1, 2001)

Grandparents' Guide to Gifted Children by James T. Webb, Janet L. Gore, Frances A. Karnes, and A. Stephen McDaniel (Paperback - Oct 30, 2004)

Mingled Roots: A Guide for Jewish Grandparents of Interfaith Children by Sunie Levin (Paperback - Mar 1, 2003)

The Granny-Nanny: A Guide for Parents & Grandparents Who Share Child Care by Lee Edwards Benning (Paperback - Apr 1, 2006)

Parents & Grandparents as Spiritual Guides: Nurturing Children of the Promise by Betty Shannon Cloyd (Perfect Paperback - Jul 1, 2000)

Grandparenting: A Guide for Today's Grandparents With over 50 Activities to Strengthen One of Life's Most Powerful and Rewarding Bonds by Sharon Wegscheider-Cruse (Paperback - May 1997)

Your First Grandchild: Useful, Touching and Hilarious Guide for First-time Grandparents by Peggy Vance, Claire Nielson, and Paul Greenwood (Paperback - Aug 1, 2009)

A Boomer's Guide to Grandparenting by Allan Zullo and Kathryn Zullo (Paperback - Aug 1, 2004)

The Nanas And The Papas: A Boomers' Guide To Grand by Zullo (Paperback - Sep 1, 1998)

Grandparenting by Grace: A Guide Through the Joys and Struggles by Irene M. Endicott (Hardcover - Oct 1994)

Solomon's Choice: A Guide to Custody for Ex-Husbands, Spurned Partners, and Forgotten Grandparents by Richard G. Kent (Paperback - Mar 25, 2006)

Intentional Grandparenting: A Contemporary Guide by Peggy Edwards and Mary Jane Stearne (Paperback - Jun 23, 2008)

49 Things In Your Home RIGHT Now That Could Harm Your Children That You MUST Be Aware Of: The Complete Home Safety Guide For Parents And Grandparents by T L Edwards (Paperback - Dec 8, 2009)

About the Author

Neil Taft is a Professional Public Speaker, tireless Youth Advocate, published author of scores of grandparents' rights articles, and a Retired Youth Minister.

Neil is the creator of the Caring Grandparents website which features articles, links, advice, and resources for grandparents who want to make a difference in their grandchildren's lives.

www.CaringGrandparents.com

S